TRUST ME

TRUST ME

FRAUDS, SCHEMES, AND SCAMS AND HOW TO AVOID THEM

GORDON G. LEEK

DUNDURN PRESS
TORONTO

Project Editor: Michael Carroll
Editor: Jennifer McKnight
Design: Courtney Horner
Printer: Webcom

Library and Archives Canada Cataloguing in Publication

Leek, Gordon G.
     Trust me : frauds, schemes, and scams and how to
avoid them / by Gordon G. Leek.

Includes bibliographical references.
ISBN 978-1-55488-705-7

     1. Fraud--Prevention. 2. Swindlers and
swindling--Prevention. I. Title.

HV6691.L36 2010   364.16'3   C2009-907533-4

1 2 3 4 5   14 13 12 11 10

Conseil des Arts du Canada   Canada Council for the Arts   Canadä   ONTARIO ARTS COUNCIL   CONSEIL DES ARTS DE L'ONTARIO

We acknowledge the support of the **Canada Council for the Arts** and the **Ontario Arts Council** for our publishing program. We also acknowledge the financial support of the **Government of Canada** through the **Canada Book Fund** and **The Association for the Export of Canadian Books**, and the **Government of Ontario** through the **Ontario Book Publishers Tax Credit program**, and the **Ontario Media Development Corporation**.

Care has been taken to trace the ownership of copyright material used in this book. The author and the publisher welcome any information enabling them to rectify any references or credits in subsequent editions.

J. Kirk Howard, President

Printed and bound in Canada.
www.dundurn.com

Dundurn Press	Gazelle Book Services Limited	Dundurn Press
3 Church Street, Suite 500	White Cross Mills	2250 Military Road
Toronto, Ontario, Canada	High Town, Lancaster, England	Tonawanda, NY
M5E 1M2	LA1 4XS	U.S.A. 14150

Mixed Sources
Product group from well-managed
forests, and other controlled sources
www.fsc.org Cert no. SW-COC-002358
© 1996 Forest Stewardship Council
FSC

This book is dedicated to my wife Debbie and my sons Garrett and Jason,
for their support throughout my policing career

CONTENTS

PREFACE

Trevor was a successful small business man in the financial planning and insurance industries. Through hard work and developing his client base, Trevor established a large network of associates and clients. One of these associates was Michael Fischer. Michael approached Trevor with a business proposition that would also benefit Trevor's clients.

Michael had developed contacts in the aircraft industry where he was able to purchase blocks of seats from different airlines at considerably lower than regular book prices. These tickets could then be resold at a profit to companies for business flights or as part of a vacation package. If Trevor would be able to get some investors together they could all take advantage of this opportunity.

Michael provided Trevor with the paperwork and the books that detailed how the block-buying worked and what the profit margins would be. Convinced, Trevor contacted ten of his clients and convinced them to invest $25,000 each. Unbeknownst to Trevor, he had unwittingly bought into a Ponzi scheme that Michael Fischer had set up. The result was Trevor and his fellow investors lost over $250,000 to this scheme.

When Trevor told me about how he lost his money he was understandably upset. However, he was not just upset about being scammed, but he was also upset on how he was treated by the police. No one appeared to understand that he was a victim. Trevor was told by the investigators he met that this was simply a bad business deal and it was therefore not a police matter.

Trevor then came to me to ask for my opinion. Although not part of the Commercial Crime Unit at the time, at Trevor's request I completed an initial investigation and report that detailed the fraud committed. Armed with this, and evidence obtained through a private investigator that Trevor hired, Trevor went back to the police, who then pursued the case.

After twenty-five years as a police officer, and before I was assigned to the Commercial Crime Unit, I often wondered how people could get caught up in these various schemes. To me, at least, they appeared to be blatant lies with nothing to back them up. Why would someone fall for this? Are these people just greedy or simply that stupid? I knew Trevor wasn't either of these things.

As a member of the Commercial Crime Unit and serving with the Alberta Partnership Against Cross-Border Fraud investigating international mass-marketing fraud cases, I had the opportunity to interview hundreds of victims of fraud. I began to realize that there is a reason why they were targeted. Most fraud victims are trusting people that would not be able to comprehend someone deliberately deceiving them. They just happened upon an opportunity presented to them that had the potential of making themselves some money. In other cases, it was a chance to help someone, whether an acquaintance, a charity, or a family member.

I also discovered that with more complex fraud schemes, nearly all of the victims had heard about the various schemes through the newspaper, television, or movies, but none of them really understood how the ruse actually worked, or how they could be or actually were drawn into the ploy.

Trust Me: Frauds, Schemes, and Scams and How to Avoid Them was written to help victims and potential victims recognize and understand how a fraud scheme works. It also explains how fraudsters select their victims and induce them to participate in their scheme and turn over thousands of dollars and life savings.

It is a sad fact of life that police departments do not have the manpower or resources to investigate most fraud cases in a timely manner, or even investigate at all if the dollar value is under a certain amount, regardless of the impact to the victim. By using case studies that illustrate these schemes, it is hoped that the reader will gain a better understanding of how a fraud scheme works, and in turn be prepared to avoid becoming a victim themselves.

As for the case involving Trevor and Michael Fischer, following a two-year investigation Fischer was sentenced to three years in jail. He has served his sentence and is currently avoiding a criminal organization that he also scammed. Trevor repaid his investors in an attempt to restore his business reputation. He was never able to recover any of the money that he and his clients gave to Fischer.

Note from the author: All references to the places and people featured in the case studies have been changed to protect the guilty and the innocent.

ACKNOWLEDGEMENTS

This is the first project of this kind that I have undertaken. It has been an interesting learning experience for me, and one that I could not have completed without the help of friends and family, for which I am truly thankful. To Johanna and Anne of Bates Literary Agency, thank you for your guidance and patience in bringing this project together. To members of the Alberta Partnership Against Cross-Border Fraud, the Calgary Police Service Commerical Crime Unit/Fraud Detail, and those fraud investigators who know that the pen can indeed be mightier than the sword. To my friends, Phil, Mark, Sharon, and Sandy, thanks for your support and comments while writing and developing this book. To my sister and brother-in-law, Jan and Bob, your insight and experience that you shared with the initial edits and drafts were great. And to my family, Debbie, Garrett, and Jason, thank you for just being there.

Gordon G. Leek
Airdrie, Alberta, 2010

[They] look upon fraud as a greater crime than theft … for they allege that care and vigilance, with a very common understanding, may preserve a man's goods from thieves, but honesty hath no fence against superior cunning … [W]here fraud is permitted or connived at, or hath no law to punish it, the honest dealer is always undone, and the knave gets the advantage.

Jonathan Swift, *Gulliver's Travels*

1

THE CONSTRUCTION
OF A FRAUD

In October 2003, Jamie Cardinal opened an account at a bank in Fort Macleod, Alberta. Two days later, Cardinal deposited a cheque into this account at the Calgary branch of the same bank. A second and a third cheque was deposited at two other branches of the bank into the same account. Two days after making his last deposit, Cardinal attempted to make a number of cash withdrawals from his account but was unable to do so. He tried again the next day but was again frustrated.

By the end of the week, Cardinal was calling the bank manager, asking why he could not access his funds and when they would be available. The manager explained that, because the cheques were from out of province, it would take a few days before the funds would be released. Cardinal told the manager that he would call him back in a few days. The manager never heard from Cardinal again. When the cheques were examined at the bank, it was discovered that they were all drawn on a company account that had its headquarters in Oshawa, Ontario. However, a closer examination of the cheques revealed more. The cheques that Cardinal deposited were "bleached" cheques and   Cardinal's name had been inserted in place of the original name. In addition to this, the amounts of the cheques had been altered.

Surveillance photographs of Cardinal making these deposits at the bank, and fingerprint examination of the cheques, all linked Cardinal to this offence. He was subsequently charged with fraud under $5,000, under Section 380(b) of the Criminal Code of Canada.

Paula was an employee of the Real Canadian Superstore in Calgary, Alberta. She would use the stand-alone bank machine, located in the foyer of the store, to withdraw cash after work. After Christmas, Paula noticed there were several cash withdrawals that she did not make. She contacted the police and claimed that someone had stolen her debit card and had taken money from her account. She did not know how this could have happened to her. In Paula's opinion, if her bank card had been stolen and used, the bank should reimburse her for the stolen money.

In the course of their investigation, the police interviewed Paula and other employees at the Superstore. The police learned that Paula had a habit of using the bank machine without taking any precautions about hiding her Personal Identification Number (PIN) from other employees. Paula was also in the habit of leaving her card on a desk in the employee common room. This provided anyone who worked for the Superstore free access to Paula's card without her knowledge.

Paula told the police that she was under the impression that the bank machine, and all bank machines, contained video surveillance cameras and the police could easily catch the culprit. The police explained to Paula that few ATMs have cameras. Without sufficient evidence to proceed with their investigation, the police informed Paula that there was nothing they could do for her. Paula resigned herself to the fact that her money was gone and that the bank would not compensate her for the loss.

WHAT IS FRAUD ANYWAY?

The crime of fraud is defined under the Criminal Code of Canada Section 380. The section reads:

380(1) Everyone who, by deceit, falsehood or other fraudulent means, whether or not it is a false pretence within the meaning of this Act, defrauds the public or any person, whether ascertained or not, of any property, money, or valuable security or any service,

    (a) is guilty of an indictable offence and liable to a term of imprisonment not exceeding ten years, where the subject-matter of the offence is a testamentary instrument or the value of the subject matter of the offence exceeds five thousand dollars; or

    (b) is guilty

        (i) of an indictable offence and is liable to imprisonment for a term not exceeding two years, or

        (ii) of an offence punishable on summary conviction,

Where the value of the subject-matter of the offence does not exceed five thousand dollars.[1]

But what does this mean to the average person? We have all had an experience that, to our minds, was definitely some sort of fraud. How does the above definition differ from what we know to be a fraud?

Fraud is an act of theft committed under special circumstances. Those circumstances are generally considered to be:

1. the person/victim was willing to part with the money, item, or service;
2. the fraudster used some form of deceit or trickery to obtain the money, item, or service; and
3. the person suffered some form of loss as a result of the trickery.

Fraud can be defined in more simple terms as "deprivation through deception," where the deprivation is the loss of the money, item, or service, and the deception is the trickery.

The problem with investigating and determining claims of a fraudulent act is that they frequently tend to straddle the borderline between a civil matter and a criminal act. To complicate this further, victims are often confused about what they consider a moral obligation and a criminal act. Because of this confusion, it may be worthwhile taking a moment to differentiate between a criminal matter and a civil matter.

Civil matters involve some form of agreement between at least two parties, such as the writing of a cheque. A cheque can be described as a contract whereby one person is saying, "I have sufficient money to purchase your item," and the other person states that he is willing to sell that item for that agreed amount.

If the cheque cannot be negotiated, or "bounces" for some reason, such as non-sufficient funds (NSF) in the account, the person who wrote the cheque has technically committed a crime. However, if it was a simple matter of poor bookkeeping that caused an overdraft to the person's account, a fraud was not necessarily committed. In legal terms, there was no *mens rea*, meaning guilty mind, or *intent* to commit fraud upon the person who obtained the cheque.

If, however, there was no money in the account, or there had never been sufficient money in the account, and the person writing the cheque knew there was no money or insufficient funds in the account, then that person has knowingly committed fraud. In this case, the person deliberately deceived the other party by implying that he had sufficient means to cover the amount of the cheque.

Moral obligations are more difficult to define because we each have our own views and beliefs on what we consider moral behaviour. Imagine you've contracted someone to repair your roof. You agree on a price and the money is paid for the repair. However, you do not establish with the contractor what quality of materials will be used, the standard to which the job will be done, or whether the job is guaranteed. You expect that the person you contracted to do the job will do the best job possible, just like you would.

After two months, and after the first rain, the roof leaks. When you call the contractor, he tells you he did the best he could. He can account for all of the money spent and the time he took doing the job. You demand that he fix the leak, but he tells you that he is too busy and the job is only guaranteed for thirty days, whether or not it rains in that time period.

Has the contractor committed a fraud or criminal act? No, he has not. All of the material and time has been accounted for and spent on the repair. Morally, should he repair the leak? Most of us would say so. Legally, can the contractor be forced to repair the leak? The civil courts would have to decide.

Often issues of fraud become confused because of the terminology used by the parties involved. Fraud victims will claim that they loaned the fraudster the money and now he won't pay it back, or that the money was to help the fraudster out by paying his rent but instead he bought alcohol or drugs with the money. These types of circumstances generally fall into the realm of civil matters. The victim has issued credit to the individual, and now must seek a civil remedy, such as small claims court, cashiering, or taking part of their wages to regain their money.

The Criminal Code of Canada section on fraud also refers to a "false pretence." A false pretence is a statement by the fraudster of a fact that is known by the person to be false or untrue. The purpose of the false statement is to cause the victim to act upon the information as if it were true. The false statement goes beyond simple exaggeration. The "statement" can be made by words, either verbally or in writing, or by deeds or actions, such as presenting a counterfeit document. We will look at some cases where the fraudster makes these statements and causes the victim to act upon these statements.

THE PSYCHOLOGY OF FRAUDSTERS AND VICTIMS

Too often fraud victims are dismissed as greedy, naïve, or just plain stupid and deserving of what they got. In some instances, this may be very true, but it is not necessarily the case for the majority of fraud victims.

Traditionally, we view ourselves as rational, logical individuals. We analyze the situation, weigh the risks against the potential benefits, and make our choices. Social psychologists, such as Carol Tavris and Elliot Aronson, believe that all of us have certain prejudices and biases programmed or "hard-wired" into our subconscious that justify our beliefs and perceptions and, at times, override our logic and judgment.

In their book, *Mistakes Were Made (But Not By Me)*, Carol Tavris and Elliot Aronson state that the brain has "blind spots" that cause us to rely upon introspection to tell us how we think and feel about ourselves and our decisions. These blind spots then allow us to justify the decisions we make based upon those beliefs.[2]

One of these biases is how each of us perceives ourselves in comparison to others. Generally, human beings have an inflated opinion of themselves. We believe that we are smarter, better looking, and more desirable than the people around us. How often have you looked at a couple and thought, "What does she see in him?" or "I have more to offer than she does." How often at work have you thought, "Without me this place would just fall apart?"

This kind of bias is a necessary part of our psychological makeup. It provides us with the confidence in our own being to try new things, to stand on our own two feet, to survive, to walk tall, and to make a difference in the world. It can also lead to overconfidence in our abilities and cause us to make incorrect decisions.

We also have the predisposition to believe what we hear, regardless of the circumstances in which we heard it. Urban legends are often considered true, even when they have been disproved. One such example of an urban legend is that of a celebrity rewarding a passing motorist for changing a flat tire or repairing their broken-down limousine. The story usually says that a motorist notices a limo stopped on the side of the road, often at night, with some form of mechanical trouble. The passing motorist stops and changes the tire or fixes a broken fan belt without realizing who the unfortunate celebrity is. Afterwards, the Good Samaritan learns that the stranded limo belonged to Bill Gates or Donald Trump, or some other rich celebrity, and the motorist was rewarded for his good deed by having his mortgage paid off.

On the surface, this story sounds like it could happen. However, when the circumstances are examined, the story falls apart. Stopping to help someone could certainly result in a reward, but paying off someone's mortgage may be a little extravagant. One might also ask why the limo driver didn't change the tire or why the celebrity didn't call for roadside assistance.

This windfall myth speaks directly to our belief that no good deed should go unrewarded. It also emphasizes the belief that sometimes you just have to be in the right place at the right time.

Phrases that begin with the preface such as "They say...," "I heard once...," or "I read somewhere ..." tend to take on a life of their own. These sayings become part of our daily speech and become established in our minds, sometimes overriding our logic and better judgment. How many of us have heard somewhere or used the axioms, "They say we all have a twin somewhere," or "I read somewhere that no two snowflakes are identical." Although none of us can say when or where we first heard this "undisputed" fact, it appears to make sense: therefore, we know that it's true.

Another adage, "A little bit of knowledge can be a dangerous thing," also holds true with regard to fraudulent situations.[3] When a person hears of various fraud schemes on the news, it gives them a false sense of bravado that again may overcome their judgment. They believe that by simply hearing of a scheme and by being alerted to the possibility that these fraudsters are out there, they now have the necessary knowledge to avoid becoming a victim.

Short news clips and exposés can only provide a sketch of a scheme and the victims it impacts. However, the viewer believes they have gained more information than they really have. By subconsciously believing that, "I have seen this on television. You can't fool me, I know all of your tricks," victims set themselves up for failure.

Other victims believe that they don't need to pay for expertise; for example, in buying and selling stocks, they think they can do it just as well as anyone. Too many people believe that they have more knowledge and experience than they really have. It is these inherent traits that fraudsters use against us to carry out their schemes.

GENERAL TRAITS OF FRAUDSTERS

When we compare fraudsters, or white-collar criminals, to others who commit property crimes such as theft, robbery, and break and enters, there are several traits that separate them from their criminal colleagues. Although not always present, the following traits are often common to all frauds, whether the fraud is committed in a business setting or targets a mass market:

> Fraudsters are often considerably older than regular property offenders, tending towards middle age. In business, they have reached a position within a company that allows them to carry out their fraud. When committing frauds on their own or as part of a group or team, they have often developed skills that will assist them in carrying out their deceptions.
>
> Unlike property offenders, most fraudsters are not interested in the adrenalin rush or thrill of the chase by the police and law enforcement, especially when it involves physical effort. They are content to take a less strenuous or less physical approach to crime.
>
> A higher proportion of fraudsters are female, for several reasons. Traditionally women have occupied the positions within a company that see them dealing with such matters as accounts payable, accounts receivable, and other clerical roles. This provides them with more opportunity to commit fraud by virtue of their access to accounts, records, and cheques. Additionally, women are in a higher proportion of positions in the retail and service industries, such as restaurants and lounges, where opportunities to access credit card information are higher. These occupational roles and types of fraud account for the higher proportion of female fraudsters.
>
> In conjunction with being older than property offenders, most fraudsters have more education than other criminals. They have at least some college education, which allowed them to obtain employment with the company in the first place.
>
> These fraudsters also have higher intelligence quotients than other criminals, which allow them to think in the abstract and to develop schemes. They know

how to operate technology with a confidence that fools others into believing that their motives are legitimate. "Spoofed" websites and the use of publishing programs to create apparent legitimate documents are just two examples of a fraudster's ability.

White-collar criminals tend to come from happier families than their criminal counterparts do. They are not generally victims of child abuse and do not come from poorer neighbourhoods. This socio-economic condition also carries through to their present circumstance, where the fraudster is often married, has a home and children, and is apparently successful both financially and socially.

From an investigative point of view, fraudsters' criminal records are generally shorter than those of other criminals. Their records will often start only a few months or years prior to being exposed in their latest venture.

In addition to having a shorter criminal record, their records will often show that several charges would have been withdrawn or minimum sentences such as probation, restitution, or conditional discharges were imposed. These minimum sentences often allow the criminal to work under the radar of law enforcement and stalk their victims.

The portrait of a fraudster, then, is that of a successful individual with high self-esteem and motivation. He or she is often kind, generous, and sociable, and comes across socially as an achiever and a doer, with a strong sense of family harmony. The fraudster also exhibits characteristics of self-sufficiency, self-control, and optimism that make him or her likeable and someone that others want to be associated with.

Although this portrait paints an individual that otherwise can be admired, the fraudster is still a criminal and a parasite, preying on the generosity and honesty of others. Their main *raison d'être* is to take from others in order to benefit only themselves.

2

BUSINESS FRAUDS

IT'S ONLY $30,000 ... THE COMPANY WON'T MISS IT

In January 1996, Debbie was employed by a large engineering company whose main clientele was the oil patch industry. Debbie held the position of accounts payable clerk for the company and had done so for thirteen years. During the period of her employment, Debbie had access to company cheques in order to pay invoices submitted by suppliers to the company.

One day in February, Debbie forged a company cheque, payable to a contracted transportation company, by printing an unauthorized cheque and forging her manager's signature. This cheque was deposited into Debbie's bank account through an ATM in addition to her regular paycheque. In March, Debbie forged a second company cheque, for the same transportation contractor, and again deposited the cheque into her account. In April, she forged a third cheque, and in June she forged two more. This pattern continued for at least nine months. The total amount of the known deposits totalled over $32,000.

In February of the following year, the chief financial officer of the company discovered discrepancies during an audit of the company's books and informed the police. The chief financial officer also stated that all but one of the cheques had forged signatures.

As a condition of her employment, Debbie had provided the company with a void cheque to her personal account to allow the direct deposit of her salary. This allowed the police to obtain a search warrant on her bank account and view her transactions. The account history showed that the cheques had been deposited through an ATM near where Debbie lived. Additionally, several other questionable deposits were noted during a review of Debbie's bank statement. Her fraudulent activities were not overly sophisticated, so upon closer examination of her records the cheques were readily traced to her. However, there was still an element of planning necessary in order for Debbie to carry out her theft from the company.

When the police confronted her, Debbie attempted suicide with an overdose of pills. When she recovered and was interviewed, Debbie claimed that her husband had no knowledge of the fraudulent cheques, even though he benefited from the additional $32,000 income. Debbie pled guilty to the fraud. Her lawyer explained to the court that she showed remorse for her actions by virtue of her suicide attempt. The court agreed with the lawyer and Debbie was sentenced to one year probation. The company had to sue Debbie separately in civil court to recoup the money that Debbie had defrauded.

THE CORPORATE ENVIRONMENT

When dealing with business fraud, there are only two areas that must be looked at in order to determine whether the company is at risk: the employees and the management of the company itself. For a company to reduce the risk of fraud, nothing is more important than promoting an ethical environment in which the employees function.

Ethics cannot be determined by laws and rules. The laws establish a minimum standard of behaviour expected by society as a whole, whereas ethics are principles that we can and should aspire to and demonstrate daily. In the business environment, ethical behaviour starts at the top and sets the example for everyone to follow.

It comes down to the simple choice between what is right and what is wrong. Are the owners, managers, and supervisors willing to lead by example and to not only "talk the talk" but "walk the walk?" If the organization is committed to a policy of integrity, fair practice, and respect, the managers, as the gatekeepers of the organization, must also practice this policy. As a manager that sets the tone of the working environment, do your employees know what is expected of them? Do your employees understand what the position of the company is regarding ethics and respect in the workplace?

It is no longer sufficient to expect someone "to know better." Not everyone has been exposed to the same environmental experiences that shape our being. Expected conduct that has been defined is mandatory for an individual to become part of the solution.

→ DEVELOPING A CORPORATE ENVIRONMENT

Organizations should have a written code of conduct which tells everyone in the organization what is expected of them. It sets a standard that is realistic and achievable. Organizations also need to spend time on educating everyone in the company what the code of conduct is and why it is so important to follow. This education should be done as part of an initial orientation and reviewed at an annual appraisal or evaluation.

When looking at the mechanics of an organization, there are a number of questions to ask to lessen the likelihood of internal business fraud.

- Is there a segregation of duties in the organization?
- Does one person control the purchasing, receivables, and payables for the organization?
- Does one person have access to organization assets and accounting records in order to cover up any dishonest activity?
- If there are no distinct personnel or department to handle all aspects of the business, are there internal controls that would prevent one

person from dishonest acts? For example: Do receiving slips have to be initialed by the person receiving them? Do the cheques have to be signed, or is there a stamp or signature machine?

- Are internal controls established and adhered to at all times? If signatures are not obtained, are there other forms that must be signed?
- If there is no purchase order do you allow items to be received or is the order checked and a replacement purchase order prepared?
- If there are internal controls, are there ways for someone to override those controls? If so, can they be changed? If there are no internal controls can potential hazards be identified? Is there someone who can monitor these hazards regularly?

In Debbie's case, the workplace atmosphere enabled her to take advantage of the business and to commit her frauds. Debbie had control of, and was entrusted with, the accounts payable. This allowed her to authorize and issue cheques to companies and suppliers. It was these bogus cheques that found their way into her account.

TAKE THIS CHEQUE AND CALL ME IN THE MORNING

Cindy was the manager for a doctor's office in Swift Current, Saskatchewan. She had been employed there for over four years and ran the office efficiently. Cindy ensured that billing for patients was sent out on time and that all bill payments were posted and deposited.

To help run the office, Cindy purchased an accounting program that allowed her to track all of the patients according to the doctor they visited, whether the payments were from an insurance claim, health plan, and so on.

After four years, the partners decided that they wanted to grow with the community and looked for investors and partners. Wanda was just what the doctors ordered. Wanda ran a chain of successful physiotherapy clinics throughout the province and felt that the addition of this office would complement her other business. Although not a medical practitioner herself, Wanda graduated with a Masters in economics and business and knew what made a successful business.

Prior to taking over the business, Wanda reviewed the books and could see that the potential for the clinic to grow was excellent. With the number of patients and the proximity to a new sports complex, Wanda and the partners had every expectation that the bottom line would be profitable to everyone.

After six months, the expected profits did not reach their anticipated levels. In fact, the clinic was losing money! This was the opposite of Wanda's experiences with her other clinics, and contradicted what the numbers should be saying. Wanda arranged for an independent audit to review the books. The audit noted some discrepancies between entries and deposits. When questioned about the discrepancies, Cindy announced her resignation and walked out the door.

Unknown to Wanda and the other partners, when Cindy walked out of the clinic, she went directly to the Health Review Board. She filed a claim stating that the clinic was double-billing patients and health insurance claims. As a result, the Health Review Board entered the clinic offices and seized all of the computer records, shutting down the business for several days. This was a classic example on Cindy's part of "the best defense is a strong offence" in an effort to deflect the investigation away from her.

The Health Board's three-month review showed that there were instances of double billing, but they were unable to determine who made the billings, whether they were deliberate, or whether they were simple accounting errors. As a result, the clinic was allowed to continue its operation but was liable to pay back the Health Board for duplicate billings.

So why was the business losing money? When Cindy first set up the accounting system and took over her management duties, she also set up a second bank account at a different bank. Cindy opened this account in her name, operating as the clinic. She did this in order to deposit cheques made out to the clinic into her own account. She also obtained a company bank card that allowed her to make cash withdrawals at the casinos she frequented without anyone suspecting her personal account.

Cindy's employers did not know that she had a gambling problem. In fact, she had been convicted five years earlier for stealing money from her previous employer in order to feed her gambling habit. In the four years that Cindy operated as the clinic's manager, she managed to skim over $400,000 into her duplicate account. All of this money went toward her gambling addiction.

In addition to the monetary loss to the company, this fraud caused irreparable damage to the reputation of the clinic and the doctors, as well as damaging family relations from the extreme pressures placed upon the partners. One doctor felt that he could no longer practice in Swift Current and moved his business to another community.

CORPORATE STRUCTURE TO PREVENT AND REDUCE FRAUD

In the case of Cindy and the doctor's office, there was no segregation of responsibilities. Cindy was responsible for the collection, recording, billing, and deposits of all money coming into the clinic. It was Cindy who bought and used the accounting program that allowed her to hide the transactions, and it was Cindy who made the actual deposits for the clinic.

Understandably, small businesses have to cut costs where they can, and sometimes margins are too tight to hire another person. This is when the owner has to decide whether to be more "hands-on," hire another person, or take his or her chances.

One of the simplest, yet most overlooked methods of fraud prevention is getting to know the people in the organization. In a small business, knowing your employees is vital. In larger corporations and institutions, it is incumbent on the managers and supervisors to display leadership by meeting regularly with subordinates and allowing them to participate in the organization through feedback and openly sharing their ideas. Those people who feel that they are part of something are less likely to sabotage it and will strive to make it succeed. It used to be referred to as MBWA — Management by Walking Around.

Most business fraudsters share common characteristics that can and should be recognizable to managers and human resources personnel. These traits can be divided into two areas: outward traits and hidden traits.

OUTWARD TRAITS OF FRAUDSTERS

Television police parlance refers to these traits as the Means, Motive, and Opportunity (MMO) for a fraudster to successfully operate within an organization. Outward traits consist of the following but are not necessarily limited to these. Fraudsters may present with all or only a few.

1. Long-term employee: This is the employee who has been with the company for many years. It used to be that when someone was hired he or she could look forward to a career that spanned twenty to thirty years. Nowadays, people change jobs and positions every five to ten years, so the concept of the long-term employee is relative. This is not saying that the long-term employee will always be looking to defraud his or her company. Fortunately, this is not the case. However, often when that same employee feels that he or she is not appreciated, or that he or she has been passed over for promotion or advancement by younger or newer members, resentment can build.

   A manager must be cognizant of this and be proactive in his or her relationships with the long-term employee. They are often the ones who made the company what it is today, no matter how minor the contribution.

2. Position of trust: Generally, the internal fraudster holds a position of trust within the organization. The person is responsible for purchasing, payables, contract negotiations, etcetera. This position of trust allows them to take advantage of the environment to their own benefit.

   Placing an extra order and keeping the balance for themselves, or writing additional cheques to themselves is not uncommon or difficult to do. This is what internal controls are meant to prevent.

3. Works overtime or never takes vacations: We have all worked overtime to complete a project or meet a deadline. When starting or expanding our business, we don't take any time off

for a vacation or take the time to look after ourselves as much as we look after the business.

Sometimes deadlines overtake us, or jobs require more effort than originally thought. This is only natural in the real business world. Valued employees who believe that they are part of the organization will more than likely put in the extra effort; either for extra pay or extra time off, or because they take pride in their work. However, not every job requires "Bob" from accounting to put in one or two hours every day after everyone else has left the building. If it does, Bob does not know his job as well as he should. A manager should ask himself whether Bob should be retrained, if any personal reasons are affecting his work, or if he's managing his fraudulent schemes, and then act on his conclusion.

A fraudster will work so much overtime because it allows him the opportunity, within their position of trust, to work on their scheme without interruption or detection. Photocopying of records, and shredding of purchase orders and shipping receipts can be done much more easily when no one is around to monitor.

Fraudsters never take a vacation because someone else may come in to cover their position while they are away, thus running the risk of having their schemes exposed. Lapping schemes and deposit skimming are two schemes that, once the fraudster is away, the systems are out of his or her control and subject to detection or collapsing. Lapping is when the fraudster continually transfers money from different bank accounts, keeping ahead of the electronic transfers and hence overlapping the funds. Deposit skimming is where the fraudster steals money and falsifies bank deposits to cover the theft. Both of these schemes will be discussed in more detail further on.

In the next case, we will see how the fraudster exhibited these outward traits and how they were eventually discovered following a company audit, and a great deal of lost money to the company.

LICENCE TO PRINT MONEY

Rupert owned a successful advertising company in Kingston, Ontario, called Hi-Def Printing. Hi-Def Printing specialized in print advertising — flyers, posters, and mailings. The company had several contracts throughout the city and area, including a couple in Ottawa and Montreal. After three years, it was time to take the next step and expand the operation.

After a substantial recruiting campaign, Larry Russell arrived as a suitable candidate to lead Hi-Def Printing into a bright future. Russell brought a wealth of experience to the position. He had been in advertising for over twenty years and owned his own smaller advertising company. Russell was able to take over the reins immediately. The shareholders met and agreed to hire Russell as the company CEO.

Under Russell's leadership, Hi-Def Printing took off. There were more contracts signed and even walk-up business improved. Russell would constantly meet new clients and take them out for lunch, paying in cash from the large roll of twenties that he always carried.

It seemed everything was moving in the direction the investors had hoped for. Then the company received a notice of non-payment to one of their suppliers amounting to several thousand dollars. This prompted a cursory review of Hi-Def Printing's finances. Although the company was busier than ever before, it was actually losing money.

The shareholders met and agreed to suspend Russell while an independent audit was conducted. The audit discovered that in the thirty-six months that Russell had been in charge of the operations of Hi-Def Printing, the company had an accounts receivable of $2.3 million and an accounts payable of $2.4 million. Russell was fired and a forensic audit was conducted on the company's books. The audit revealed that Russell had used the company's income to supplement his own business and personal lifestyle.

Russell's base salary as CEO was agreed upon as $85,000, plus expenses. In the first year, Russell paid himself a bonus of $150,000 over and above his salary. In addition, Russell's expense account actually equalled his base salary.

Russell had used Hi-Def Printing to sub-contract the contracts to his own smaller company, and then billed Hi-Def Printing for the amount, which was often for more than what was agreed upon. He also constantly purchased supplies and equipment for his company through Hi-Def Printing, and had them delivered to his company, sometimes "forgetting" to send the inventory to Hi-Def Printing.

The audit also showed discrepancies with the cash deposits. When a client paid in cash, the paper bills were initially deposited into a safe in Russell's office. The coins, on the other hand, were put into a large "Texas-Mickey" bottle that Russell kept beside his desk. This bottle served as the petty cash for the company.

Russell would make the cash deposits at the bank a few times a week; however, the cash billings rarely balanced with the deposits. In addition, these deposits were always for even-numbered amounts: $350.00, $425.00, $500.00, and so on. An audit of the receipts showed that the amounts should have been more likely $387.53, $442.37, and $573.86. In other words, Russell was skimming deposits from Hi-Def Printing. On average, $1,500 was skimmed from the cash deposits every month. The cash deposits only matched the bills and receipts during the times that Russell was away on holidays and the assistant manager took over the bank deposits.

The audit also uncovered double billings on Russell's expense account for lunches, several with the shareholders of the company, and a more luxurious car than what had been agreed to by the company. There were external expenses that the audit was not able to confirm or track back to the company's expenses.

Russell had recently purchased a new house in an acreage cul-de-sac, complete with swimming pool, game room, home theatre system, and a three car garage where he parked his luxury car. He also held an annual block party for his neighbours with free food and liquor, and also sponsored an annual golf tournament for friends and clients — all expensed to the company.

HIDDEN TRAITS COMMON TO FRAUDSTERS

Hidden traits are just what they sound like. They are events and happenings in the fraudster's life that fellow employees or managers may not be aware of. When colleagues learn that an individual defrauded the company, invariably everyone says, "I should have known something was wrong," or "She had changed after her divorce," or "I always wondered how he was able to afford that house," and so on.

The following traits are often indicators or triggers for fraudulent activity. These traits do not always indicate fraudulent activity, but if there is a problem, they may be a starting place to look.

1. Living beyond one's means: Does the person live in a house or condo that is unrealistic or inappropriate in relation to their salary? Do they drive an expensive import or luxury vehicle or take extravagant and exotic holidays? Russell lived in a large house and held extravagant parties for friends and neighbours.

2. Change in personal circumstances: Has the person recently been divorced or lost someone close to them? Often a drastic change like this will cause that person to take a chance or take risks just to "feel alive."

3. Emotional instability: As with a change in personal circumstances, being diagnosed with a disease or depression will also cause a person to do something that otherwise would be totally out of character or unexpected.

4. Drug or alcohol problem: Does the person show up at work hung-over or late? Drug and alcohol problems and the effects on family and work have been substantially documented. They will not be covered in this book, but they may be an indicator of fraudulent activities in conjunction with other signs.

5. Gambling: Gambling is recognized as a mental illness that needs treatment. When interviewing fraudsters who had gambling as the root cause of their frauds, they claimed that it was like being in a different state of mind. They did not know what they were doing or how much money was being lost. Gambling became an

addiction that they could not control. Any conscious thought about the amount of money being lost, or where the money came from, became irrelevant.

6. Dissatisfaction: Has the person been constantly passed over for promotion or recognition? Have they received credit where credit was due? Was their performance that which is expected of a good or long-time employee?

These traits are not legal defences for committing fraud, although these issues may be raised by the defence attorney in court. However, some of these traits may be how the fraudster justifies their actions to themselves and to allow the fraudster to act "out of character." Getting to know one's employees is the single most effective way for an owner or manager to prevent fraud and other incidents, either criminal or socially inappropriate, in the workplace.

In the case involving Hi-Def Printing and Larry Russell, Hi-Def Printing lost over $850,000 as a result of Russell's activities. Russell was charged with theft for the deposit skimming, and fraud for the double billings on his expense account and purchases of supplies made for his own company and billed to Hi-Def Printing. The amount of money attributed to the criminal theft and fraud charges was approximately $80,000.

The other expenses that Russell racked up — his bonus and new car, etcetera — did not lead to Criminal Code charges due to the vagaries of Russell's contract with Hi-Def Printing. The recovery of these expenses had to be determined in a long and separate civil court action.

3

TELEMARKETING FRAUDS

Cross-border telemarketing and mass-marketing fraud is one of the most pervasive forms of white-collar crime in Canada, the United States, and the world. Telephones and the Internet eliminate borders and allow unequalled communication with potential victims. These tools, designed to allow free and unrestricted communication, are a criminal's best friend.

Internet fraud has steadily increased in the last three years: 31 percent in 2000; 42 percent in 2001; and 47 percent in 2002.[1] The 2004 International Conference on Identity Theft claims that identity theft alone costs Canadians an estimated $2.5 billion per year: $100 for every man, woman, and child in Canada.[2] Cellular phones, prepaid calling cards, and 1-800 numbers increase mobility and eliminate the need for a structured base of operations. This unrestricted access creates jurisdictional issues in intelligence gathering and enforcement which challenge both governments and police agencies.

Legitimate businesses rely on mass marketing to lawfully target potential customers for their products. This mass marketing takes many forms: television, radio, newspaper and magazine advertising, bulk mailing, telemarketing, and the Internet. It is estimated that mass-marketing efforts result in a 1 percent success rate. What this means is that 1 percent of all potential consumers will respond to direct marketing advertising.

So, in order for companies to remain competitive in today's increasing global market, the consumer pool must be flooded. Hence, the increase in telephone marketing and computer "spam" that inundates us daily.

Although inconvenient at best, the value of mass-marketing techniques cannot be dismissed. The effectiveness of telephone marketing has coined its own phrase for all similar forms of mass marketing — telemarketing and, as a result, telemarketing fraud.

TYPES OF CROSS-BORDER TELEMARKETING FRAUD

There are many telemarketing scams, with new ones being invented daily. The PhoneBusters website lists twenty-six common scams, from lottery and prize pitch scams to false charities, pyramid schemes, identity theft, and phishing, just to name a few.

The PhoneBusters National Call Centre estimates that between five hundred and one thousand "telemarketing boiler rooms" are operating in Canada daily. "Boiler rooms" are a group of individuals recruited to call potential consumers and offer them a scripted pitch to purchase a product.

In *Fleeced!: Telemarketing Rip-Offs and How to Avoid Them*, Fred Schulte explains the telemarketing pitch:

> The telemarketing pitch is built around three themes. The first strategy is to find a means to make the victim feel special. That is why so many phone offers use a prize gimmick or other come-on that keeps the customer on the line. Stage two quickly follows and is simple enough: make the mind work. The marketer misleads the buyer into thinking the product is first rate. The third ingredient of the telemarketing sale is urgency. The deal is always "good this day only" or "only a few are left and they soon will be gone."[3]

Stock investment and precious gems and metals schemes historically have used these tactics successfully. However, loan schemes are starting to become more prevalent and are able to capitalize on the consumer.

It is tempting to categorize the victims of these schemes as greedy individuals who get what they deserve. Although a certain element of greed must be acknowledged, telemarketing fraudsters play to a person's emotions. Their "winnings" will help them to retire, provide for their grandchildren, or help others who are less fortunate in some war-torn African country. As one victim who lost $4,800 on a lottery scheme commented, "I am not usually this gullible. But these people win your confidence. My three grown-up children will be horrified."

There are as many pitches as there are criminals to invent them. Recently, prize money and lottery schemes, loan offers, low interest credit cards, or credit card protection scams have increased substantially.

Prize money and lottery schemes generally take the same format. A victim is contacted and told that they have won the Australian, Canadian, or Spanish Lottery, and they will receive official confirmation in the next few weeks. Next, a letter, which appears legitimate, arrives from a law firm stating that they are acting as agents for the lottery corporation. The wording and titles are chosen to sound familiar and therefore legitimate to the recipient. The letter states that to avoid paying exorbitant taxes on the person's "winnings," they can pay the taxes of the country where the lottery took place.

Once the "hook" is set and the funds are promised, criminal telemarketers persuade their victims to use an electronic transfer of funds because of the anonymity that this allows them. Victims will wire funds through a legitimate business, which does not follow the same reporting and recording guidelines that financial institutions must follow. A victim will be instructed to use a cash outlet, such as Money Mart or Western Union, to wire funds to the fraudster. The fraudster will then show up at the outlet and claim the cash. Usually, the fraudster uses a false name and fake identification to claim the cash.

In other instances, the victim will be instructed to mail a cheque to a post office box or "drop box" leased by the fraudster. These are often leased for a six-month period, under a false name and paid in cash.

After six months, the fraudster just walks away from the drop box and sets up a new address.

In some more extensive schemes, fraudsters will also use couriers to pick up mail at their drop boxes and forward the cheques to a second or third address. These addresses are often in a different city or province than the one where the victim sent the cheque.

The use of drop boxes and the extensive use of multiple couriers make the tracking of activities difficult. Even if the fraudster's courier is intercepted, often the courier's only knowledge is that he was hired to pick up and deliver, or re-route, an item from a mailbox. Although he or she may be part of the overall scheme, generally their involvement and knowledge is minimal and will not lead to the main fraudster.

One confidential police informant provided the following description of how these types of schemes work. This is an extract of an interview he gave on a lottery scam that colleagues of his had been operating in Red Deer, Alberta:

> I know a lot of people who do what they call [the] Elgordo Scam. They rip off more than $200,000 or more a week. One of the [big-time organizers] for this scam is Prince Salop and his sidekick is Sophia and the other associate is Ursa and more associates that work for him. His business starts from 7 am to 4 pm from Monday to Friday.
>
> He has people come over to his house and they get a calling card and they start calling people from the United States. They have a long list of leads [phone numbers] they call per day. They have more than twenty potential victims per day. When they call people they tell them they are calling from Spain. They give the victim a toll-free number and tell them to call tomorrow morning. They will transfer their file to a financial company in Toronto. The next day the victim calls stating they won money. That is when the scamming skills come into play. Victims send in a certain amount of money for security deposit and they run off with the money.

There are five phases to [this] scam:

1. Opening calls with potential victims;
2. Making customers submit sample money (maybe a small fund);
3. The IRS scam (making customers send a second fund) [This is a scam within a scam to have the victim pay taxes and allegedly fool the IRS];
4. Once a customer has already sent a sample money order, they have a choice then to send more money;
5. If they cannot send the large sum of money, Prince negotiates a deal with the customer that he will send a cheque to the customer (which is a false cheque). They send the cheque and they do a follow up on the cheque and Prince makes the customer trust him by telling the customer that they will split the cheque, (once the customer cashes the cheque).

The names for these scams are telling as well. Elgordo means "the fat one" in Spanish, a comment on how these fraudsters view their victims. There are also popular music videos circulating in Nigeria and on the Internet that make fun of fraud victims and venerate the fraudsters who take advantage of them.

The concept of telemarketing fraud is not new. The scope and the tools used may be evolving, but governments and law enforcement are becoming more educated not only of the mechanics involved, but also to the devastation and toll that this type of fraud takes upon its victims. For a victim, $100,000, $200,000, or more represents their life's savings. These victims do not have another lifetime to build up their savings again.

HERE I COME TO SAVE THE DAY

Helen is an eighty-five-year-old widow living in Kansas. At some time previous, Helen had lost an unknown amount of money through a fraudulent telemarketing scheme in which she was informed that she had won the Australian Lottery. For a fee, the fraudsters would forward her winnings to her. Of course, after she paid into this scheme, no monies were forthcoming.

In October, an individual who identified himself as James Buchanan contacted Helen. He purported to be an agent for Internal Fraud Investigations, a company that allegedly recovers money for victims of telemarketing frauds. Helen was again talked into providing money to help finance the expenses of International Fraud Investigations in an effort to retrieve some of her lost funds.

This scheme is commonly referred to as a "recovery pitch telemarketing scheme." In this recovery scheme, previous victims are often put onto a list that is sold to other telemarketing fraudsters. This list is referred to by various names: sucker list, mooch list, etcetera. These previous victims of a telemarketing scheme would then be contacted to participate in other schemes such as the Spanish/Australian/Canadian Lottery, investment opportunities, or, as in this case, be convinced to spend additional funds to help the fraudsters pay expenses in retrieving their stolen money.

Victims of recovery pitches seldom question how the fraudsters got their name and information, or how they knew of their previous loss. Often they simply assume that the company somehow is working with the police and that is how and why they were contacted.

The strength of this scheme is that most seniors are afraid to tell family members that they have fallen prey to a scheme in the first place. They believe, or are convinced by the fraudster, that if they tell someone they will be considered unable to look after themselves and incapable of making sound decisions. This is secondary victimization, which often has a greater impact than the actual monetary loss because it attacks the person's sense of independence and self-worth.

Alleged representatives of this recovery company continually contacted Helen. One of the individuals identified himself as Edward Truman, the president of the company Progressive Strategy. At some point during these conversations, Helen was informed that the "parent company" was Allowance Assembly International (AAI) in Calgary.

The names provided to the victim were those of former presidents of the United States or other names that had a familiar sound to them. A familiar-sounding name provides an air of legitimacy and familiarity to the victim. He or she feels that they know, or at least have heard of, the person and, by default, the organization that they represent. Therefore, it must be true or legitimate.

In late October, Helen sent Allowance Assembly International a cheque in the amount of $20,000 in U.S. dollars. In November, Helen sent AAI a second cheque in the amount of $40,000 U.S. The addresses of both companies were mailbox outlets.

In December, a woman who identified herself as Jackie Brown contacted Helen and stated that she could help her recover her money. Brown left a number and asked Helen to send a cheque for $15,000. In this instance, Helen did not send the money.

Meanwhile, a second victim, eighty-three-year old Walter, was being contacted by a person identifying himself as John Hallaway. Hallaway informed Walter that he was a representative of Internal Fraud Investigations and that he was conducting an investigation on behalf of over two hundred people who had lost their money to phony lottery scams. If Walter was interested in being part of the investigation, he would need an initial investment of $60,000 to cover expenses, lawyer fees, and so on.

Walter told Hallaway that he did not have that kind of money, but Hallaway convinced Walter that he would make an exception in his case and include him as part of the investigation for only $43,000. The remaining money that Walter would "owe" him would come out of the money being recovered. Walter was instructed to make the cheque payable to Allowance Assembly International, the parent company of Internal Fraud Investigations.

While Walter and Helen were trying to recover their money, a third victim, seventy-nine-year-old Norma, was also contacted by someone identifying himself as Michael McKenny. McKenny claimed to be an attorney investigating Canadian lottery frauds as was currently being shown on the news and various documentaries. McKenny claimed that he was launching a class-action suit against the Canadian Lottery

Corporation in an attempt to recover victims' money, especially for those victims like Norma, where seniors have no other support.

McKenny managed to convince Norma to send a cashier cheque for $65,000 to defray the legal cost. Norma was advised that the cheque should be made to the parent company of McKenny's law office, Allowance Assembly International, and that he or other representatives would be in constant communication with her.

The police executed a search warrant on the bank account where the cheques were deposited. As a result of the search warrant, three other victims were identified: Iris, Margaret, and Melvin, who were all trying to recover their money.

HOW HUMAN NATURE IS USED AGAINST US

Human nature is a wonderful thing. It allows us to be generous to those less fortunate and it pushes us to achieve our goals and dreams. However, human nature can also be predictable. This predisposition allows a General to plan his strategies and operations, a marketing strategist to prepare targeted marketing campaigns, and a fraudster to plot his or her schemes.

One of these predictable tendencies is how we view losses and gains. Our human nature makes us tend to weigh losses more heavily than gains. We often judge ourselves more harshly after a loss or a poor score on a test, while accepting a win or a perfect grade as only natural in the course of our lives. This skewed thinking can be severely problematic for some. Instead of seeing prior losses as unrecoverable, victims continue to engage in risky behaviour in the small hope of recovering something. This is part of the psychology behind gambling and so-called gambling addicts.

Think about the last time you were at the fair and you played one of the skill games to win a stuffed animal. After four, five, or six tries, you make a decision to either stop or continue on because "you almost had it the last time." Finally, after even more attempts, you are rewarded with a small consolation prize that you convince yourself is worth the $45 you spent winning it. Carnival operators know that our human nature will make us keep trying to win that prize.

In the book *Influence: The Psychology of Persuasion*, Dr. Robert B. Cialdini lists six universal principles of why people say yes:

1. Reciprocation: Providing something after being given a gift or favour;
2. Social Proof: Establishing that others are doing the same thing;
3. Authority: Establishing personal expertise or credentials;
4. Scarcity: The desire for something rare or of limited availability;
5. Commitment and Consistency: Obtaining a commitment based upon a person's previous convictions; and
6. Liking: People will do things for those they like.[4]

In a scheme like this one involving Helen and Walter, today's telemarketing fraudster will take the time to build a rapport with his victims to get to know them and their families. In Helen's case, Truman built a personal background that included his wife's operation for breast cancer, his two sons graduating and moving on to college, and he even sent a picture (not of himself) of the family vacationing (an example of liking). Hallaway asked Walter about his ailments and sent him a get well card when he was in the hospital for a short period (reciprocation). James Buchanan claimed to be an agent for Internal Fraud Investigations (authority), while John Hallaway informed Walter he was conducting an investigation on behalf of two hundred people (social proof).

All of these ploys and deceptions are to build up the confidence and trust of the victims. In interviewing victims of fraudulent telemarketers, investigators have found that victims always say how nice and pleasant the fraudster was. "He didn't sound like a criminal," or "She always asked how my daughter was doing, or my grandchildren."

Another ploy fraudsters may use is to give low-cost gifts to reinforce the image that the victim has won something or is gaining (reciprocation). How many small prizes were given to you before winning that large stuffed dog? Fraudsters also frequently play on the victim's honesty, good name, and personal word. This tactic, expressed as commitment and consistency by Cialdini, is especially effective with older generations, who remember when a handshake and your word were good enough to seal a deal. When employing this ruse, the fraudster will make a promise and then give his word, but would want your word back. He would then question your integrity by asking if he can trust your word. When the answer is yes, then the hook has been set.

On one end of the criminal scale, fraudsters are often looked upon as "not really criminals." They're "just" white-collar criminals targeting greedy people or large corporations that can afford to lose or part with the money. What they're doing isn't really hurting anyone. In the cases of banks and insurance companies, well, that's why we pay those charges and interest rates.

In reality, fraudsters are calculating individuals who follow a pre-determined structure in order to gain an advantage over their victims. As in a cult, the confidence and charisma of the fraudster entices his followers into doing exactly what he wants and needs them to do.

UNDER PRESSURE

In September 2004, Gail and her friend Jessica were looking for a part-time job after school. After reading the classified ads, one position appealed to them. It was close and seemed fairly easy. The ad read:

> Earn money in your spare time
> Telephone sales personnel required immediately
> Training provided and bonuses paid for performance
> Call Mike at 555-1234

Gail made the call and an interview was set for her and Jessica the next evening. Upon arriving at the office, the girls were greeted by a receptionist, who introduced them to Mike. After a brief interview and the signing of papers, Mike told them they were hired. The girls were introduced to a couple of other employees who would be their coaches and answer any questions they may have.

Gail sat down with Janice, who explained the procedure to her. The company, Reliability Savings International, provided credit cards to people unfortunate enough to be turned down by the big banks. The company utilized a database that they purchased from a marketing company, and contacted the potential customers to whom they provided the opportunity to own a credit card.

Janice went on to explain that there was a script to follow when calling people, and that the numbers and clients were printed on coloured sheets of paper corresponding with the various time zones in the United States. Gail was provided a desk, computer, and telephone headset. She sat, watched, listened, and learned how Janice made her calls.

> My name is Janice. I'm calling you from MasterCard. About three months ago you applied for a MasterCard with a $5000.00 limit, but were turned down. I'm with Reliability Savings International and we are willing to provide you with a MasterCard with a $2000.00 limit. There are no monthly fees and there is 0% interest for 3 years. The only cost to you is a one time fee of $249.00 and this money is directly debited from your chequing account. [*sic*]

Once the potential client agreed, the call was transferred to the account manager, who would complete and process the paperwork.

After listening to a few calls, Gail thought that she was capable of making the calls on her own. She was provided with her list and began calling numbers from the yellow sheets. Gail learned that yellow corresponded to Pacific Time and, as such, was two hours ahead of her local time.

After several calls, one of the customers began to ask some questions of Gail and the company. Gail read the prepared material that Mike had given her: "Reliability Savings International is a multi-faceted organization interested in providing deserving clients with financial assistance and means to achieve their goals. We offer financial advisors and investment opportunities worldwide."

When the client asked where the company was located, Gail answered that she was located at the head office in Saskatoon, Canada. At this moment, Mike was walking by Gail's desk and overheard the conversation. He immediately disconnected the call and sent Gail into his office. Once inside, Mike explained to Gail that she was never, under any circumstances, to give the location or telephone number of the company. If clients needed further information they were to be transferred to him or Janice.

Gail returned to her desk and made several more calls, but decided that she was not going to come back the next day. Something didn't feel quite right to her. On the way home, she and Jessica decided that they both had enough, and would look for another part-time job. The next day, Jessica still had the feeling that something was wrong and she decided to call the police.

These fraudsters operate what is commonly referred to as a boiler room. Such an operation can be described as a series of telephone and computer lines originating in one location to conduct mass marketing or telemarketing. The victims, once contacted, provided bank information to employees of Reliability Savings International.

In this scheme, the Reliability Savings International telemarketers made representations to the victims using various pitches, notably that they were able to provide the victim with a major, pre-approved credit card with a $2,000 U.S. limit. The advantage to this credit card, so the victim is told, is that there are no monthly fees, and no interest for three years. Once the victim agrees to purchase the credit card, the Reliability Savings International representative advises that there is a one-time "processing fee" of $249. They then obtain two pieces of identification and banking information, including a chequing account number. The victim's bank account is then debited the $249.

Victims of such schemes do not receive a credit card, only applications for prepaid credit cards (which require an additional payment of $39.95), brochures, coupons, or nothing at all. These same victims are often put onto a list that is sold to other telemarketing fraudsters. These victims would then be contacted to participate in other telemarketing schemes.

Reliability Savings International was actually part of a larger telemarketing organization with other boiler rooms located in the Toronto area. In addition, the scheme called for mail drops and processors of the banking information to be located in Florida, New

York State, and Quebec. The leaders of the organization lived in the United States and Ontario — using people like Mike to set up and run their satellite operations.

The casual observer might say that the money being collected is very small ($249) and these victims should have known better, but we must not lose sight of the larger picture. Although the initial amount is small, if one calculates one week in the Saskatoon boiler room, where two hundred people are defrauded, multiplied by eighteen months, the boiler room operation took in $3.5 million. The Toronto boiler rooms would take in ten times that amount.

A vast majority of the people who fall prey to this type of scheme generally are desperate to establish credit for a variety of reasons. Some are young people starting out in life after finishing school, some are widows whose husbands managed all of the financial arrangements, while others have been victims of identity theft. These people, and others like them, will attempt to obtain a legitimate credit card in order to function in today's world.

In addition, businesses are also victimized by these schemes. The effect on the reputation and the cost of business to banks and credit card providers can be severely damaged. In turn, this may result in additional costs for security passed onto everyday consumers.

→ BOILER ROOM TRAITS AND COMMONALITIES

Gail and Jessica had bad feelings about the company when they first walked in; nevertheless, they decided to give it a chance. When responding to ads like Gail and Jessica did, there are a few points to consider in helping to determine whether the company is legitimate or not.

Does the ad include an address for the company or simply a telephone number to call? These organizations survive by being difficult to locate. At most, a post office box will be all that is provided for an address. Often the phone number provided in the ad will be a cell phone number, making it difficult for the authorities to track down the key players.

At the location, does the business give the impression of being permanent and legitimate? Is the company's name on the door or on the office index in the foyer? Are the windows covered so that passers-by cannot look in? Do the facilities, desks, and telephone offices have a look of permanency or are they simply put up with wires running everywhere?

Finally, when talking to clients, are you instructed to give vague answers or lie about where you are located? Are there lots of cash "bonuses" being paid to high performers? All of these things can add up to an illegal telemarketing boiler room.

If you find yourself involved with or suspect that you are participating in an illegal boiler room, be aware that you may face criminal charges if you continue to participate. If you are not charged, you may be called as a witness in court against the individuals running the boiler room.

4

LOAN SCHEMES AND ADVANCE FEE FRAUDS

EVERYONE APPROVED (FOR A PRICE)

Mike lived in a small community a few hours outside Kamloops, British Columbia. He was married and his children were attending college. The community, although not large, boasted its own business district, local newspaper, and community centre. After twenty years of working for others, Mike saw an opportunity to purchase a small business where he could work for himself. After being turned down by his personal bank, Mike began to look at other options for acquiring a loan.

Some of his friends advised him that they had heard of loan brokers who didn't have the same restrictions that banks do for individuals. After all, banks were only interested in lending money to larger companies or established businesses, not the little guy trying to start up a business. Mike began looking in his local paper in the classified ads and came across an ad for personal and small business loans. The company, Equity Financial Group, listed a business address and several phone numbers. Mike called and spoke to the company's chief financial consultant, Bob Rosi.

Rosi was sympathetic to Mike's position and said that he had heard the same thing from many of his clients. All they want to do is improve their family's fortunes and they get turned down by the big banks. Rosi took some information and advised Mike that he would send him some forms and documents in the mail.

When the forms arrived, Mike completed them, providing his Social Insurance Number, personal banking information, and employment records, and returned the forms that day. Mike then received a call from Rosi advising him that Equity Financial Group had approved Mike's loan application for $180,000. However, they would require an upfront fee of $6,000 in order to secure the loan. This could be paid by certified cheque, money order, or wiring the funds. Mike did not feel comfortable sending this money to someone he had not met so he drove into town to meet with Rosi. Rosi suggested to Mike that, instead of meeting at the company office, why don't they meet for coffee or lunch? Mike agreed and he met with Rosi at a Tim Hortons, where he signed a contract and gave Rosi a certified cheque.

Equity Financial cashed the cheque at a local financial institution before Mike had made the drive back home. After three weeks, Mike still had not received his loan. When he called to inquire about the status of the loan, Rosi advised Mike that there were some problems processing the funds, but the money would be released within a day or two. After another week, Mike called again. He was met with a recorded message that the number was no longer in service.

This scheme is referred to as an advance fee loan scheme. An advance fee loan scheme requires that the person seeking a loan pay an up-front processing fee to the financial institution that is providing the funds for the loan. In 2003, there were over 2,900 reported American victims of telemarketing loan schemes like this one, with an average loss to these victims of $1,100.[1] Usually, the ads appear in the classified section of a newspaper. More recently, these ads are appearing in the local papers of outlying communities in order to escape the radar of police departments.

Bob Rosi learned how to complete frauds after meeting his mentor, Goldie Bowen. Bowen had been charged and convicted of several petty crimes, including theft and fraud spanning fifteen years. It was Bowen who implemented the scheme to set up a company offering personal and small business loans to individuals who were unable to obtain credit from other sources.

Bowen leased a small office in south Calgary and took an ad in the Yellow Pages. She then put the same ad in the local paper, paying in cash for both the office and the ads. As her business became successful, she brought Bob Rosi on as a front man for the company. Meanwhile, she expanded the newspaper ads to the surrounding communities. Often, she would change the name of the financial company in order to make it more difficult to connect it to her. Bowen also brought in Harlan Bruce, an associate familiar with accounting principles and procedures, to create false financial statements for her victims, to show how profitable Equity Financial Group was and that the money which these "investors" put into the company was secure.

After Bowen was arrested and charged with this scheme, Rosi decided to go into the business on his own. He had moved to British Columbia and placed ads in the papers between Saskatoon and Vancouver. Rosi would lease a mailbox and use this as the mailing address for his place of business. If the loans were for a smaller amount — $20,000 to $50,000 — Rosi would "approve" the loan within a day over the phone. The victim would be told that a processing fee of $1,500 had to be sent before the money would be released. Often the would-be victim would become suspicious and not send money, but in enough cases Rosi would receive his fee and the victim would not hear anything.

Like most fraud schemes, advance fee loan schemes appear to walk the tightrope of legitimacy. The pitch sounds reasonable to the victim on the surface. Generally, there is nothing illegal about an advance fee loan, provided the funds are available, and the individual gets his loan. Although there may be an issue with high interest rates that can be viewed as criminal rates, if the applicant gets his money after paying the fee, very little police follow-up will be done, unless there are extenuating circumstances. However, in most jurisdictions, it is illegal for a company to request an upfront fee prior to obtaining a loan.

Low-interest schemes attract business people looking for investment opportunities when they have been turned down by established financial institutions, while credit card protection schemes offer consumers insurance and low interest rates on credit card purchases. However, all of these schemes have the same three elements: make the person feel special, make the mind work, and show urgency.

If you cannot get a loan through traditional lending institutions, it is unlikely that you'll get one in response to a classified ad. One precaution would be to ask the loan company to take the amount of their fee off the total amount of the loan that was promised to you.

5

FRAUDS THAT TARGET INDIVIDUALS

I AM A PLAYER NOW

After finishing work selling cars, David headed off to his favourite restaurant for some dinner and a few drinks. David liked the popular downtown nightspot because it gave him an opportunity to mix and meet with other professionals. At thirty-five years, David had big plans for himself and was working towards what he called his "five-year plan."

David wanted to be in marketing and promotions. He had already met and struck up an acquaintance with a couple of nightclub owners, laying the groundwork. All he needed was to make the right connection, and he would be well on his way.

When he entered the club, he noticed that the restaurant was full. He saw a place at the bar in the lounge so he made his way over, sat down, and ordered a rum and coke. Sitting beside David was a well-dressed man in his mid-thirties. His short black hair and dark complexion made David think of European or Mediterranean descent. When the man ordered a drink from the waitress, David detected a slight English accent. David had not noticed him in the lounge on previous occasions and, always being on the lookout for a potential opportunity, would have made note of this gentleman.

The man introduced himself to David as Dr. Santos Coffman and said that he had just arrived into town from London, England. Santos had recently come into an inheritance and bought a partnership with Angle Recording Studios in London. He was here to scout out some local but unknown talent that he could sign to a recording deal. He was also interested in possibly making a few investments into the local nightclub scene. Perhaps David would know of someone?

David could not believe his good fortune. This was the break he was looking for, and just like in the movies, it was happening to him because he was in the right place at the right time. David told Santos of his plans to work in the promotion industry and that he could introduce Santos to a few friends of his that were looking for an investor for their nightclub. David also had a line on a blues singer whom Santos might be interested in hearing, Big Motha Mike. After a few more drinks, and a couple of phone calls by David, the two agreed to meet the next night.

The following night, David introduced Santos to Jack and Duane, two partners in a downtown nightclub. The club had been running for six months, but as Jack explained to Santos, it needed an influx of capital to make some repairs and upgrades. Santos agreed to look over the club and, seeing that it was only two blocks from the main nightclub district, agreed that the club did have the potential to be a major draw. Santos agreed to invest in the club as a one-third partner. If Jack and Duane would draw up the papers, he would meet with them the next day and present them with a cheque.

Also playing that night at the club, through David's arranging, was Big Motha Mike. Santos listened attentively. When the set was over, he agreed with David that this was the type of sound he had come looking for. Santos met with Big Motha Mike and offered to sign him to a four-year contract with Angle Records in London with a retainer of $250,000.

The next night, Santos met with Jack, Duane, and David back at the original restaurant. They ordered drinks and a celebratory dinner to seal the deal. Upon signing the contract, Santos gave Jack a cheque for $250,000 to become a one-third partner in the nightclub. Santos did not forget David, either.

As a token of his appreciation for introducing Santos to Jack and Duane, Santos gave David a cheque for $10,000 and asked if David would be interested in being hired on contract as Santos' marketing manager. David readily agreed and ordered a bottle of champagne to celebrate.

Unfortunately for David, Jack, and Duane, there was more to Santos than met the eye. Dr. Santos Coffman, whose real name was Parker Clement, had arrived in Calgary about two weeks before meeting David. He had just completed eighteen months in a B.C. correctional centre for fraud and selling false stocks. Once he was settled in his residence and after checking in with his probation officer, Coffman/Clement began to look for a job that would help him in his new home.

Clement applied for a counselling position with a social services agency. During the interview process, Clement claimed to have a degree in psychology from Dalhousie University, with a minor in business administration. He also claimed to have extensive experience in counselling troubled youth — probably drawing on his own personal experience. When asked for documents to support his qualifications, Clement explained that after two days in the city, his car had been broken into and his briefcase was stolen. However, he had already asked for copies of his diplomas and should be able to provide them within a few weeks.

Once hired, Clement then went to work on his real job of creating his new persona. He practiced writing the name Dr. Santos Coffman and his initials until it was free flowing. He then purchased business cheques online, with the corresponding software to produce business and personal cheques. Finally, he utilized the Internet to purchase false European identification.

Clement was a typical fraudster in that he had more than one scheme going at the same time. Besides portraying himself as a high roller and nightclub investor, he also presented himself as a knowledgeable broker in the stock market.

Clement frequented the nightclubs of the East-Indian community, where, due to his good looks, he was able to meet plenty of young women.

He would then explain that he had opportunities to purchase stocks and that this would be a good investment for them. Clement would provide projections and monthly statements to substantiate his claims and to quell any concerns his victims would have.

Unfortunately for Clement, all of his various schemes began to collapse around him at the same time. The fraudulent cheques he had given to David, Jack, and Duane were drawn on a non-existing account and failed to clear the banks into which the cheques were deposited. Regrettably, Duane and Jack had already written cheques to suppliers to have a new roof put onto the club, and for the teardown and construction of a new interior for the club. Consequently, when Clement's cheques bounced, so did everyone else's.

When some of Clement's investors failed to find the stocks on the various stock exchanges, they wanted their money back. Of course, Clement was unreachable by phone or through his address. The investors were left with useless pieces of paper.

As for the documents provided to his only legitimate employer, several spelling mistakes on his "diplomas," and forged signatures on other documents, eventually gave him away. Clement's diploma claimed that he had a "Bachlor in Major in Business Administration." He also had a second diploma claiming that Clement had a "Bachlor in Minor in Psychology." We often read and see what we expect to see, passing over what later appears to be glaring errors. In this case, it took six weeks before the administration noticed the incorrect spelling of "Bachelor" and the wording on the diplomas. As well, Angel Records exists in London, but not Angle Records. Someone who was involved in the entertainment industry should have noticed this mistake.

Clement failed to show up for work so that he could be fired. Instead, he was arrested and pled guilty to the charges, receiving two years in jail.

What Clement had relied on for his first scheme was the desperation of his victims and their lack of business skills. People like David, Jack, and Duane often overlook subtle signs because they believe that the fraudster is genuine. The money that is being offered is coming at just the right time so other considerations are often overlooked. In David's case, he believed that he was a more sophisticated financial advisor than he really was. David had the desire and the ability, but not the experience to recognize that he could be duped by someone like Clement.

It has always been a wise practice to do your research when entering into any business venture. The use of the Internet, Voice over Internet Protocol (VoIP) telephone services, and other media can literally provide a world of potential opportunities and hazards. Today, it is even more important to "look before you leap" when accepting business partners. Legitimate investors will be happy to provide contacts and references. Talk with your bank manager or financial advisor. Often they can perform a financial check that will at least tell you if the person you plan to deal with is legitimate.

As for buying stocks from someone out of his briefcase, again a small amount of due diligence on the part of the victim would have saved these victims a lot of grief. An Internet search of companies and stocks will quickly show if they are available, and whether this is a worthwhile investment. Do not get caught up in the "limited time opportunity." It's been said before, "You want a good stock tip? Don't listen to stock tips."

THERE'S ONLY YOU

After thirty-three years, Brent had decided it was time he should get married. When Brent met Lacey, he felt that she was the girl for him. The two began dating. Eventually Brent asked Lacey to marry him, and she accepted. To begin setting up their home, Brent gave his fiancée his debit and visa cards, along with his PIN, in order for her to make payments at his bank while he was working. Unknown to Brent, Lacey had other ideas.

Lacey used Brent's debit card and credit card to withdraw money from Brent's account so that she could go partying. Lacey also acquired several of Brent's personal cheques, which she made out to herself for cash, so that she had what she called "pocket money." Brent was not aware of Lacey's spending until the bank contacted him about missing some bill payments. It wasn't the only thing that Brent was not aware of.

Before she met Brent, Lacey worked as an apprentice electrician for a small electrical business in the city. The business was owned by Patricia and her daughter Elizabeth. Lacey would do minor electrical work and run errands for Patricia when she needed supplies picked up. Because the business office was operated from Patricia's home, Patricia had a habit of leaving the company credit card on her desk, in order to keep it handy for paying couriers.

On several occasions, Lacey would take the credit card and treat herself to dinners and drinks at the local pub. She would also get cash advances on the credit card, for pocket money, when she was out at the bar with friends. Lacey would often sign Elizabeth's name on the credit card receipts and return the card to the desk.

After a few months, Patricia was reviewing the books. She saw several bar tabs that she did not recognize. Patricia called the credit card company and asked for copies of these receipts. When they arrived, Patricia saw that Elizabeth had apparently signed for the tabs. Patricia knew that Elizabeth did not usually frequent the area where the bar was located, and she suspected that Lacey was behind the bills. When Elizabeth and Patricia confronted Lacey, she quit and stormed out of the house.

Meanwhile, while Lacey was engaged to Brent, she was also living with another man, Mathew. Mathew and Lacey had been living together for a couple of months, although there was never any talk of marriage. During the time that she was with Mathew, Lacey had stolen one of his chequebooks and wrote several cheques to herself from Mathew's account. Mathew was not aware of his missing chequebook until Lacey went away for a holiday.

As there was no firm commitment between Mathew and her, Lacey took the opportunity to accompany another boyfriend, James, to Prince George for a couple of weeks. While James was attending business meetings, he would let Lacey use his truck for the day. Lacey would also use his credit cards. Whenever James began looking for them, Lacey would always manage to "find" them between the seats of the truck or in James' other pair of pants. On one occasion, she also stole cash destined for the bank from James' briefcase, altering the deposit slip to escape detection and James' notice.

While engaged to Brent, living with Mathew, and travelling with James, Lacey also found the time to apply for a credit card in the name of another boyfriend, Rodney, with a supplementary card in her name. Lacey completed the application and had the cards sent to her mother's address. Lacey was able to obtain a total credit between these two cards of $10,000.

When the bills and phone calls from credit companies began to arrive, Brent, Mathew, James, and Rodney went to the police. They would have confronted Lacey, but she had already moved on to other things.

After her falling out with Brent, *et al*, Lacey met up with her long-time boyfriend, Chris Collins. Chris and Lacey had a scheme where they would advertise vehicles for sale on eBay. The listing contained a picture of the truck and described the work that had been done. Chris would advertise the truck and he would get several offers.

One such offer was from Todd from Virginia. Todd enjoyed buying and fixing up trucks, and then showing them at various car shows. This truck, a 1967 Ford, was one that Todd had always liked the looks of. He was very disappointed when he was told that the bidding had been closed. Fortunately, two days after the bidding closed on the Ford, Todd was contacted by Lacey, who told Todd that the purchaser of the truck backed out of the deal. She and Chris were wondering if Todd was still interested in buying the truck.

Todd couldn't believe his good fortune and agreed to the purchase price of $6,500, plus $1,500 to cover shipping costs. Lacey explained to Todd that they had an account established with a financial company that specializes in foreign exchange, and gave the details of wiring the money. Todd made arrangements to wire the money to Canada, and waited to get his truck. After four weeks the truck still had not arrived, so Todd called Lacey and Chris asking if there was a problem. Chris explained that the truck was still in customs but should be released within a day or two.

After two more weeks of waiting, Todd again called, but this time he did not get any answer. When Todd called eBay security, he was informed that the transaction was outside of eBay's control because the sale was completed after the bidding. They couldn't help him. Todd then called his local police department.

Unknown to Todd, Lacey and Chris had completed this scam over twenty times on victims across the United States. By targeting American victims, and completing the sale after the closing bids, Chris and Lacey knew that eBay would not investigate them. As a result, instead of one investigation linking all of the victims to the pair, there were several smaller reports in various states.

Most of Lacey's frauds were straightforward, using a credit card or cashing cheques and forging signatures. What this story, and Clement's, illustrates is that most fraudsters have more than one scheme going on at the same time. When discovered, the different schemes aren't often connected and are treated as separate and distinct occurrences, with different victims' and different methodology. It fails to give the whole picture and the scope of the frauds being committed.

As one of the largest retail operations in the world, eBay has developed procedures designed to protect the consumers and the sellers registered. If, as in Rick's case, consumers choose to make purchases outside of these procedures, then eBay is not responsible for any fraudulent transactions. However, they will cooperate with any investigation to the best of their abilities, while keeping the information and profiles of their clients confidential.

When using Internet services such as eBay, follow the rules and you'll likely not have any regrets. When you step outside the safeguards established by these companies, you become very vulnerable to unscrupulous people.

When you purchase items online, make an attempt to find out about the seller. Get a phone number and address that you can call back and check on, in case there is a problem with your order. Conduct an online Internet search and see if there have been any unsatisfied customers, or if the person has been selling lots of items. Although not necessarily conclusive, the information will help you make a more informed decision. Remember, a legitimate business person should be happy to show that they are legitimate, and that they are trustworthy.

Lacey was charged with several counts of fraud and theft involving the use of the credit cards and cheques and stealing cash. She pled guilty to some of the charges and received a six-month sentence, to be served on weekends, and a $1,500 fine. Chris and Lacey were also charged for twenty-three counts of fraud each regarding the eBay truck scheme. Most of these charges were withdrawn because witnesses were unable or unwilling to travel to Canada to attend court, and the numerous states where the victims lived made extradition of Chris and Lacey unfeasible.

MARRIAGE PROPOSAL

Juliet was a middle-aged, single, professional woman living in the city. She owned her own condo, her vehicle, and had managed to put a sizable amount away for her retirement. Her friends considered her attractive, and her fellow employees considered her dependable and caring. Juliet was a nurse at the hospital and as such worked shift work. This made it difficult for Juliet to meet other people and "doing the bar scene" was not really her thing.

One Sunday, while reading the paper, Juliet came across a personal ad that caught her eye:

> Single male looking for friendship and companionship with intelligent single female. Must be caring and a good conversationalist.

Juliet could not say afterward what it was that made her decide to call, but she thought a phone call couldn't hurt anything. She called the number listed and met Chase.

Chase Pike was a charming gentleman on the telephone. He had a quiet voice and told Juliet that he was a bit older than she was, in his mid-fifties. He worked for one of the airline companies and was also a part owner in a moving company that caused him to be away a lot of the time. He cared for his sister, an invalid who could not leave the house. She's the reason he placed an ad in the paper, to meet someone like Juliet.

The relationship went on for several months. It progressed from phone calls to meetings for dinner, and eventually talk moved towards marriage. Juliet and Chase began to look at building a new house to share their life together.

One Saturday, the couple located a new development for upscale condominiums that appeared to suit their needs. They met with the developer and arranged for a $20,000 deposit on their new condo. As Chase's money was tied up in the moving business, Juliet agreed to write a cheque for the deposit. As the weeks and months went by, Juliet was looking forward to moving into their new home.

One day, Chase came to Juliet's home and informed her that the developer had declared bankruptcy. As a result, they had lost the $20,000 deposit that they had put on the condominium. Chase told Juliet that he went to the developer's head offices and argued and shouted with the owner and their lawyers, but to no avail. Juliet was devastated. Chase comforted her and assured her that things would work out for the two of them.

A couple of weeks later, Juliet and Chase were again looking at new homes and discussing possibilities. It was then Chase told Juliet that he had an opportunity through the airline to purchase shares for $15 a share. Chase showed Juliet the business section of the local paper and explained how the stocks of the company were currently trading at $22 per share. Chase described to Juliet how he could purchase 5,000 shares and roll them over in a couple of weeks for a profit. They would regain what the crooked developer stole from them.

Juliet was a bit skeptical, but it seemed to make sense to her as Chase explained it. She was sure that she had heard how employees of large corporations get inside information in advance of the general public and are able to make a good profit. Chase had explained that he had to be the one to make the investment because he was an employee. That way everything would appear to be above board and legal. As Chase's funds were still tied up in the moving business, Juliet provided the $30,000 to Chase.

After making the investment, Juliet and Chase's relationship began to cool. Chase seemed to be constantly away in other provinces with his moving company, and rarely saw Juliet when he was home. He did call her two to three times a week, but it just wasn't the same. Finally, Juliet decided she couldn't carry on this way. She was going to break her engagement to Chase. Juliet had never been to Chase's house before, but she located the address in the telephone book. Gathering her courage and putting her emotions in check, Juliet drove to Chase's house.

When Juliet rang the doorbell, the door was answered by a woman in her mid-forties. Juliet wasn't surprised; after all, Chase had told her that he cared for his handicapped sister. This woman showed no signs of any incapacity. Juliet introduced herself as Chase's fiancée and stated, "You must be Chase's sister. Chase has told me about you."

The woman replied, "I am not Chase's sister. I am his wife."

The two women stared at each other until Chase's "sister," Barbara, told Juliet to come inside and explain herself. Inside the home, Juliet began to tell Barbara the events of the past year. While she was doing this, Chase walked into the house and joined the two women. This was more than Juliet could stand. She began to cry and accuse Chase of cheating her and lying to her. Finally, Chase stood up and told Juliet that she had to leave his house, she was upsetting his wife. Juliet fled from the house and drove back to her home.

As it turned out, Juliet was not Chase's only victim. Chase's story was a lie from the moment he placed his ad in the paper. Chase had an extensive record for fraud dating back to the 1960s, when he had spent time in jail for fraud offenses. He was not in his mid-fifties but was actually sixty-nine years old when he met Juliet. Nor did he work for an airline, although his moving company appeared to have been a real asset at one time. The charade that Chase performed with Juliet as his victim had also taken place with other attractive, intelligent, middle-aged women.

Barbara, Chase's "sister," had also met Chase through a personal ad in the newspaper. After a whirlwind romance, Chase and Barbara got married. He was still operating his moving business, but the recession caused some unforeseen business expenses. Chase convinced Barbara to give him $50,000 to meet these expenses for the short term. Afterward, Barbara learned that Chase had really used the money to pay off his previous debts and his ex-wife.

Chase had been married four times before Barbara met him. In the latest instance, Chase met June, once again through a personal ad in a newspaper. June was also a caregiver who worked various shifts and had difficulty meeting people. June and Chase had a romance that culminated in marriage and a honeymoon in Mexico, paid for by June. When the couple returned home, Chase moved back into his own residence and did not live with June. After two weeks, June filed for divorce. Chase's other three marriages followed the same pattern.

Chase Pike is a parasite who preys on vulnerable, lonely women. His pattern is such that he answers personal ads in the newspaper to meet vulnerable women to achieve his ends. Unfortunately, these lonely, and to their minds desperate, women fall for his stories and are taken advantage of. They are often too embarrassed to report these instances to the police, feeling that they are at fault. Efforts to locate other victims are often frustrated by the known victim's reluctance to go public. Fraudsters like Pike count on these traits to continue with their lies.

For the record, Pike took back the money originally given to the developer within a week of the down payment, and vanished, as did the money for the stock options that Juliet provided. Had Juliet been a less caring individual, and been more willing to treat her financial arrangements with Pike as a business venture, perhaps she might have avoided losing her home and savings.

When dealing with money and assets, always consult an outside party, such as a lawyer or investment broker, who can provide guidance and protection. Prenuptial agreements are often derided by couples, but they can serve a valuable purpose.

WHAT YOU SAID IS NOT WHAT I HEARD

Francis had been living with her boyfriend for a little over a year when they decided to break up and go their separate ways. Francis was twenty-five years old and had a steady job at a store in the mall. Without her boyfriend, however, rent and other bills were going to be tight.

Francis looked on the Internet and discovered a site listing potential roommates. After reading several of the entries online, she decided to settle on one that appeared to meet her needs. The ad stated that Janice was twenty-four years old. She was being transferred to Regina from London, England, and her company was willing to relocate her. Janice went on to describe herself as a non-smoker, enjoyed hiking and camping, and liked to listen to jazz music.

Francis thought that Janice sounded like the ideal roommate and contacted her through her e-mail account. Janice replied the next day, and thought that she would be able to move within the next month. Francis informed Janice that the rent would be $800 per month, plus her share of the utilities, which would likely be another $150. Janice thought that this sounded reasonable and would have her company send her a cheque to cover expenses and to seal the deal.

A short time later, Francis received a cheque from Janice's company, St. Andrews Golf and Resort, with an address from Toronto, Ontario. The cheque was made out to Francis but was for the amount $23,950. Surprised, Francis contacted Janice and asked her what was going on, and why the cheque was for so much money. Janice explained that, with her transfer and relocation, the company obviously made a mistake. The cheque sent to Francis was supposed to cover the first month's rent and utilities, $950. The company was to issue a second cheque for $23,000 to cover other expenses that Janice might encounter. Five thousand of the $23,000 was supposed to be sent to Janice's grandmother in the United States. According to Janice, her grandmother was undergoing an operation, and this money was to offset the hospital costs that were beginning to grow.

Janice was so sorry that it was such an inconvenience for Francis, but asked if she could do her a favour. Would Francis be willing to deposit the cheque into her account and wait for it to clear? Then Francis could keep the first month's rent and send the balance of the cheque back to her. Janice suggested that it would be better if Francis kept the first month's rent and a damage deposit as well, especially for the inconvenience that this was causing her.

Francis decided that she would agree to deposit the cheque; after all, it was a company cheque and she knew about St. Andrews Golf and Resort. Besides, if it cleared the bank, what would her risk be? Francis went to her bank, deposited the cheque, and went away for a week to visit some family.

After ten days, Francis called her bank and asked her if the cheque she deposited from Janice had cleared. The bank told Francis that the cheque had cleared. Upon hearing this, Francis wrote Janice a cheque for

$16,250, keeping $950 for the rent and an additional $800 for the damage deposit, and sent Janice's grandmother a cheque for $5,000.

Three days later, when Francis tried to withdraw some cash from her account, she was unable to do so. Her account was overdrawn by almost $22,000. When Francis went to the bank to find out why she could not access her money, she discovered that "cleared" and "hold" mean different things, and that Francis was responsible for reimbursing the bank for the money she sent to Janice.

The cheque that Francis received from Janice's company is known as a forged cheque or bleached cheque. Sometimes it is also called a counterfeit cheque. This terminology is wrong because the only thing that is considered counterfeit, with respect to fraud, is money. A forged or bleached cheque is a legitimate cheque that has been altered, by various means. The cheque amount and the payee are changed so the fraudster can deposit the cheque into a bank account or forward the cheque to an unsuspecting victim. When the victim gets the cheque, it is usually for an amount greater than what was expected. The fraudster will come up with a reason for the large amount that sounds plausible to the victim. The fraudster will instruct the victim to deposit the cheque, keep the amount that they are owed, and usually a bonus for the inconvenience, and send the balance back to the fraudster.

Unfortunately for Francis, she didn't understand the terminology used by her bank. To her, a cleared cheque was the same as having the money in her account and available. To the bank, a hold and cleared are two different things. When a cheque is deposited into a bank, it is forwarded to a clearing house that will review the cheque for non-sufficient funds, closed accounts, or other instructions that may be on the account. It does not necessarily ensure that the cheque is authorized by the account holder. The cheque is then forwarded to the account holder's bank for processing.

A hold is typically when the bank is waiting for the funds to actually arrive at the bank from the account that the cheque was written against. Your account may actually show the funds deposited into your account. However, these funds will generally not be available for your use until the hold is lifted and the money has been made available from the account that the cheque was written against. Unfortunately, these two terms are often used interchangeably and cause confusion to those of us who are not familiar with the nuances of financial terminology.

The only time the money in your account belongs to you is when the bank has been credited, or paid, by the account holder that the cheque was drawn against. This is also referred to as having the cheque honoured. Always ask the bank if the cheque has been honoured and if the bank has been credited the funds. If it has not, do not touch the money.

Much like reading the fine print on a contract, we are responsible to understand the terminology of banks and other financial institutions. Ask questions and find out about the bank's policies for deposits and withdrawals. Whether there was a breakdown in the bank's protocol for detecting counterfeit cheques is immaterial. Francis was still held responsible to replace the money she sent on Janice's behalf.

VEHICLES FOR SALE: GOOD CONDITION, LOW MILES, MANY OWNERS

Melissa owned a 1995 Toyota Camry for ten years. It was not her first car, but it was her favourite, with all of the optional features that she could get put into it. She enjoyed driving the car through the mountains and taking it on summer drives, but with her business, it was no longer a practical vehicle.

Melissa drove into Red Deer, Alberta, where she came across a used car dealership — Cars-4-You. The sign advertised trades and consignment vehicles with on-site financing available. Melissa was not really planning to buy a new vehicle that day, but a 2003 Chevy Silverado in the lot was just what she was looking for. She pulled into the lot and was met by a salesman, Karl Cervantes.

Cervantes had been in the car sales business for over thirty years. He had worked in Alberta, British Columbia, and Saskatchewan. He was very successful and was known throughout the industry as a hard-working go-getter. While other salesmen would wait for clients to come into the lot, Cervantes would scour the papers and call people offering to sell their vehicles on consignment. Cervantes' specialty was high-end luxury vehicles.

Cervantes took Melissa to the Chevy and showed her all of the features: crew-cab, air conditioning, and power locks and windows. Everything imaginable on a truck appeared to be here. For only $28,000, it was a bargain. Melissa fell in love with the truck and agreed to the contract. She consigned her Toyota to Cervantes and drove off with her new truck. She had it registered in her name and was happy with her purchase.

The Chevy Silverado was not Cervantes' only sale that day. Madeline had her Lexus that she wanted to consign, and Jeremy had his Mercedes also on consignment. Cervantes was able to sell these vehicles for the asking price of $35,000 and $42,000 to two families that had driven in from Calgary.

Two months after Melissa bought her truck, she received a call from the Royal Canadian Mounted Police, asking if she owned a 2003 Chevy Silverado. Melissa said that she did and the Mounties asked if she would come into their office to talk. When Melissa arrived at the police station, the Mounties explained that the truck was consigned to Cars-4-You, but the owner had never received payment for the vehicle. Melissa produced her bill of sale and registration and explained that she had bought the vehicle in good faith from what she believed was a reputable dealer. The Mounties agreed but advised that she may be contacted in the future.

At the same time, other purchasers and consignees of Cervantes were being questioned by the police and being asked to provide copies of bills of sale and registration for the vehicles they now possessed.

In a three month period, Cervantes had sold over forty-five vehicles on consignment, averaging $30,000 each. The owners who had put the cars on consignment were not contacted by Cervantes when their cars sold and did not receive any money from him. The purchasers of the cars believed that they had bought their vehicles in good faith and that they now owned the vehicles. Meanwhile, Cervantes had not been seen for the past two weeks.

Although not a hard and fast rule, purchasers of a vehicle who produce a bill of sale and registration are generally deemed the owner of the vehicle. However, in the case of consigned vehicles, the original owners may still be considered the legal owner in a civil court, even though the new purchaser has paid the intermediary. It makes for a messy, agonizing situation for everyone.

When selling a vehicle on consignment, ensure that you do your homework and use the following guidelines:

1. Find out about the reputation of the dealer and read the contracts that you are given. Contact your provincial consumer services office or the Better Business Bureau. With the widespread use of the Internet, it is possible to learn whether people have had problems with specific dealers or companies.
2. Don't be afraid to follow up on a regular basis and drive by the dealership to ensure your car is still on the lot.
3. If you purchase a vehicle, even on consignment, conduct a lien check before purchasing. If there is a lien on the vehicle and you still purchase it, it is more likely you will lose the car should something go wrong.

In the case with Cervantes and his victims, three people who had their vehicle sold on consignment were able to get their vehicle back after hiring a lawyer and going to civil court. The other victims were unable or unwilling to spend the time and money to go to court, and therefore lost their vehicle and the money for which it was sold for. As for Cervantes himself, his whereabouts were unknown. Arrest warrant applications for forty-eight charges of fraud were applied for as well as charges under provincial legislation with respect to operating a car dealership. Six months after the charges were filed, a confidential informant notified the police that two of Cervantes' victims had tracked him to Toronto, where they took matters into their own hands and assaulted him with baseball bats. The next day Cervantes took a flight to London, England, and has not been heard from since.

6

FALSE CREDENTIALS AND THE ART OF DECEPTION

TRUST ME, I'M AN ACCOUNTANT

Sebastien Vinesh moved to Edmonton from Montreal in the late 1970s. Vinesh had been involved in the drug trade, mainly cocaine, and after some trouble in Montreal he decided to move west and start again. Most of Vinesh's customers were part of Edmonton's gay community, and, being gay himself, Vinesh was more than willing to deal with the community. Another part of Vinesh's makeup was that he was interested in accounting and could be quite successful at it.

One August, Vinesh met Julie at a nightclub he always frequented. Julie was married to George, the owner of a moderate oil and gas exploration company. Julie was not there with George that night; instead, she was looking to score some cocaine. It did not take long for Vinesh and Julie to get acquainted, and Julie became a regular customer of Vinesh's.

After several months of supplying Julie with cocaine and learning about George's business, Vinesh proposed that, since he was a chartered accountant, he could do George's books for him for less money than

George was probably paying now. This would also allow Vinesh to keep in contact with Julie and keep her cocaine supply available. Julie proposed this plan to George, who reluctantly agreed to Julie's wishes. It wasn't long before Vinesh convinced Julie and her sixteen-year-old daughter Samantha that he could do more work for George's company if he moved into the spare basement suite.

By this time, George was aware that Julie had a drug problem and he suspected that Vinesh was the source. He also suspected that Vinesh was also providing cocaine to his daughter. However, George did not want to create a scene that would upset Julie, so he allowed Vinesh to move in and hoped that his support would be enough to see them through this.

Vinesh continued as George's accountant, paying the bills and completing the ledgers. To George's surprise, Vinesh was quite good at accounting. Vinesh had purchased, through the company, an accounting software program that enabled him to fulfill all of the basic accounting needs. This, along with his natural ability, allowed him to give the appearance of a professional accountant.

After two years of Vinesh living in her home and providing her and Samantha with cocaine, Julie was tragically killed in a motor vehicle accident. After the funeral, George felt that he had no further obligation to maintain Vinesh and had him move out. He also arranged for Samantha to undergo treatment for her drug addiction. Everything appeared to be getting back on track — until the bills started coming.

While acting as George's accountant, Vinesh had applied for a credit card for himself in George's company's name without George's knowledge. With this card, Vinesh purchased two cell phones; one for himself and one for his partner. He then took a skiing vacation to Whistler, British Columbia, with his partner, and booked a separate spa retreat in the United States, again with his partner, and advanced himself $5,000 cash to pay for other "incidentals."

George made several attempts to locate Vinesh but was unable to track him down. He made the decision to reimburse the company from his personal funds and to drop the whole affair. In his mind, the cost of the trips and the cash were the price he had to pay to get Vinesh out of his and Samantha's life — until Vinesh cashed a $20,000 cheque drawn on the company. George's business partner insisted that he call the police, and Vinesh was charged for the frauds against the company. Following the laying of criminal charges and after pleading guilty to the fraud and theft charges against George, Vinesh was released on probation and was once again free to move on to his next victim.

Le Sorbonne d'Edmonton is a full-emersion French school in an affluent neighbourhood in Edmonton, Alberta. The school caters to families whose lifestyle involves travelling abroad and working in other countries. The school is governed by a board of directors and raises money through pledges and donations as well as tuition. The accountant for the school had decided that it was time to retire and take time for himself. The school therefore approached a local personnel agency, Blackwell Personnel, to provide them with an accountant.

Blackwell had what they believed was the perfect candidate. He was French-Canadian, had a degree in accounting from McGill University, and had several letters of reference. The school agreed, and Sebastien Vinesh was dispatched to the school to meet the board. The board was suitably impressed with Vinesh's credentials and agreed to hire him. The previous accountant agreed to stay on for a month to aid in the transition.

After the previous accountant's departure, Vinesh took over control of the school's finances. To do this, he insisted that he needed complete control over banking functions: writing cheques, making deposits, petty cash, and the handling of donations. To assist the school, Vinesh donated the purchase of an accounting program that he was familiar with.

Vinesh ingratiated himself into the daily happenings at the school. He donated $50 to the school's fundraising efforts for the victims of natural disasters and he offered to count and deposit the funds from the cafeteria. However, Vinesh was also a gossiper. He began to spread lies and innuendos about various members of the staff, especially when their role brought them into contact with his financial responsibilities. He would also use his homosexuality as a weapon against staff members, claiming that certain people did not like him or were against him because of his gay lifestyle.

The situation came to a head when $4,500 that the students had raised for disaster relief failed to be deposited into the bank. Vinesh claimed that he had seen one of the teachers outside his office the day before and that he did not trust her because of some of the rumours going around. These were the same rumours that Vinesh had started weeks previously.

The board decided that the missing money was a matter for the police to investigate. Vinesh promised his full cooperation, but left that evening and was not seen by the board again.

When the police investigated the incident, they discovered a number of holes in Vinesh's life story. Although he was French-Canadian, he had never attended McGill University, let alone graduate with an accounting degree. The letters of reference had all been produced by Vinesh's partner, and produced on manufactured letterhead to fictitious companies in Quebec. The accounting program that he donated to the school was one of two that he had used the school's credit card to purchase; in effect, making the school donate it to themselves. It was the same program he had used when working for George's company, so it was no wonder he was familiar with it. As for the $50 donation, this was the difference in the petty cash that another teacher had counted and then Vinesh deposited. Police examination also revealed that there was no sign of forced entry into Vinesh's office or filing cabinet where the $4,500 was kept prior to the theft.

Unfortunately, Vinesh was not finished with his adventures. A land development company hired him, while using the same references he used for the school. Again, Vinesh insisted that he have sole control over the accounting and finances, and he began to spread dissent throughout the office once again. Vinesh was so successful in this endeavour that he was able to convince the managers to move the safe containing stock documents into his office and to make him solely responsible for the combination.

Vinesh used his position at the development company to pay for another trip to Whistler for him and his partner, to repair his car, to make purchases over the Internet, and to obtain two more cell phones.

Vinesh's house of cards came down when one afternoon the travel agent booking his flight to Hawaii called the development company for authorization and left a message with one of the managers. This manager confronted Vinesh, and in an indignant rage, Vinesh submitted his letter of resignation and walked out. Once he had gone, the company discovered his use of the company credit card to finance all of his purchases. They also found that several blank company cheques had gone missing. These turned up as counterfeit cheques to be deposited into the United States, but there was no direct evidence to tie Vinesh to these cheques and the matter was not investigated further.

Vinesh next went to work for a manufacturing company as their chief accountant. Again, he was able to convince the owner to provide him with control of the accounting and signing authority for purchase orders and accounts payable. Vinesh also attempted to continue with his pattern of divide and conquer by spreading rumours about the staff. Fortunately for the company, the manager also happened to be the owner's daughter, Michelle.

One morning, Michelle received a call from a local car dealership telling her that the company's new Mustang convertible was ready for pickup after its regular servicing. This was a surprise to Michelle. She drove an older model Honda and knew nothing about a new Mustang. When she asked the leasing company, she was told that Vinesh had leased it in the company's name six months ago. Michelle knew that something was not right and began to review the accounts payable ledgers. Her reviews led her to some interesting discoveries.

Besides the Mustang, and all applicable registration and insurance, Vinesh had authorized five $2,000 bonuses within two months. He had purchased office furniture and an alarm system for his personal residence, and also purchased two laptop computers, two cell phones, and other miscellaneous items over the Internet. Michelle was prepared to confront Vinesh and had arranged for the police to be present to arrest him at the office. Not surprisingly, Vinesh failed to come into work that day or any day after. He was busy outside the city.

Vinesh met Sandra and Jim Hodges when he was looking to purchase a car for his partner. Jim and Sandra owned a small used auto parts lot specializing in Ford Thunderbirds. Like most small businesses, they had a select clientele and were moderately successful. A deal was struck to sell Vinesh a Thunderbird for $4,000 and for the use of his accounting services.

Vinesh had confided in Jim and Sandra that he was planning on moving to Drumheller with his partner to open a restaurant. He hoped that he could make it work just like Jim and Sandra had made their business work. Over the months, Vinesh was a frequent visitor to the Hodges' house and auto yard doing the books and striking up a friendship with them.

One evening, Vinesh showed up at the house unexpectedly, needing to speak to Jim. Vinesh had just learned of an opportunity to purchase a site for his restaurant. It was available for $125,000, but the deal would not last because it was a prime location. Vinesh wanted to offer Jim a special deal, because he needed the cash quickly. Vinesh explained that when he was working for a land developer, he had had the opportunity to buy some share certificates from a family whose father died, and they had missed several payments. Vinesh had purchased seventy-five thousand shares and did not want to sell them, but he needed the cash right away. Vinesh went on the Internet and showed the stock market report of the shares currently trading at $1.35 a share. Vinesh was willing to sell them to Jim for a total price of $60,000.

Although Jim was not familiar with the stock market, even he knew this was a good deal. Even if he sold them next week, since today was Friday and the markets had closed, he would make a profit. The deal was done on a handshake, and Jim wrote Vinesh a company cheque for $60,000.

Over the next several months, Vinesh would contact Jim, but not as frequently as before. On one occasion, Vinesh told Jim he needed another $10,000 for restaurant renovations, but his accounts were tied up. Could Jim loan him the money for no more than a month? Jim agreed and wrote Vinesh another cheque for $10,000. Finally, the calls from Vinesh stopped all together. Jim and Sandra carried on with their business but wanted to expand with a specialized workshop and tools. It appeared to be a good time to cash in the shares they had purchased from Vinesh, so they went to the developer's office.

Once inside the manager's office, Jim and Sandra offered to sell their shares to the company for the current market value. The manager examined the share certificates and realized something was wrong. He knew the owners of the certificates and also knew they had not sold them.

It appeared that the certificates were stolen from the safe that was in their former accountant's office and were still the property of the original owners as there was no transfer of title to the Hodges. He told Jim and Sandra that the matter was out of his hands and should be referred to the police.

When presented with a deal that appears to be too good to be true, it often is. If someone offers an exceptional return on an investment, take the time to do some research. Deals are rarely so time sensitive that they have to be acted upon without some thought or simple precautions. Remember that the fraudster wants you to act quickly and impulsively because the longer you take to think about his or her offer, the more likely that his or her scheme will be discovered.

When trusting someone like Vinesh to handle and manage your money, take the time to check all references and call the companies in question. If presented with stocks and certificates, contact the company issuing the certificates or the holder's name on the certificate. Ensure that the certificates are legitimate and that the person is actually acting on behalf of the company.

Most fraudsters are more than capable of coming up with, and juggling, numerous schemes and obtaining money from their victims. They can provide all the documents, diplomas, references, and anything else you may ask for in order to forward their scheme. It is all based and founded on a lie. Like any weak foundation, once it starts to crumble, the rest of the structure will tumble down.

If the personnel agency had checked the references more closely, they would have noticed that Vinesh's reference contact information was the same as his home address. If the companies that Vinesh worked for had recognized the disharmony that was occurring in the office, they could have been alerted sooner to potential problems. If the Hodges had made inquiries about purchasing and selling certificates with a financial advisor, they may not have handed over their money so quickly. Of course, hindsight is always "20/20."

You don't have to distrust everyone or expect that everyone is out to rip you off, but like comparison shopping, it pays to be informed. And although a little knowledge can be dangerous, a reasonable amount of knowledge is your best defence.

7

INVESTMENT SCHEMES

I ALWAYS WANTED TO BE A SECRET AGENT: AGENT "00 NOTHING"

Buck still lived on the farm that his grandparents homesteaded seventy years ago. The farm had been parcelled off and rented to other ranchers in the area, but Buck still maintained the four acres that held his house, barn, and a few other outbuildings.

Buck was introduced to Timothy Morgan through his insurance agent, Michael Chase. Chase explained to Buck that Morgan would be taking over several of his clients, as he would be going away for a while. Morgan was heavy-set with thinning hair but was able to talk to Buck about farming, the lack of rain, and the price of cattle in a manner that put Buck at ease. Morgan seemed to have the knowledge about farming into which you had to be born. Purchasing insurance from him seemed to be a natural thing for Buck to do.

After getting to know Morgan for a year, Buck was surprised to learn that Morgan was no longer in the insurance business. As Morgan explained, there were a lot of young up-and-comers who made it difficult for someone like Morgan to be competitive. The companies now didn't want their salesmen to get to know their clients like Morgan did. They wanted their employees to sign them up and move on to another client. Morgan had had enough of that, so he decided to get into the development business. As Morgan took the time to explain to Buck, there were lots of opportunities in today's burgeoning real estate market. With his connections, Morgan knew that he could do very well for himself and for his friends, as Buck had come to be over the past year.

Morgan was working on a real estate investment that promised to be very lucrative, if Buck was interested. Pinnacle Land Development was building a new community west of the city, and Morgan was able to purchase half a dozen lots from the land owner, Simon Ratherson. Simon was in his eighties now and spent most of his time in Florida, as he didn't like to deal with the Canadian prairie winters anymore. Morgan showed Buck the site plan and the proposed subdivision and some of the pictures that he had taken of the land already being cleared. If Buck was interested, he could buy into the deal for $50,000.

Buck was intrigued. It was true that development was going crazy, with the city encroaching on the outlining towns. Farming was getting to be too much work for him now that he was on his own, and his daughter had no interest in the land. This would be a tidy nest egg for her. Buck called his bank, arranged for a loan on part of his land, and presented Morgan with a cheque for $50,000 the next week. Morgan was careful to explain to Buck that this was an investment that would come due in about two years as people bought their land parcels. Buck said he understood that it would take time to earn a profit and agreed to the deal.

As the months went on, Morgan was able to offer Buck the inside track on a couple of other deals he had going. Through his connections in real estate development, he made contact with some overseas investors. As a result, Morgan was currently working with the Nigerian National Petroleum Company, developing off-shore oil wells. Morgan showed Buck his letters and contracts from the Nigerian government and copies of the letters of credit from the Nigerian National Bank.

He also had the actual certificates showing that the potential for this investment would be in the neighbourhood of $23 million. Would Buck want in on this deal as well?

It seemed like a good deal with unlimited potential. However, Buck was skeptical. He had heard about Nigerian scams on the news. Morgan assured him that those schemes involved getting those get-rich-quick letters and faxes. However, if Buck wanted to just put in a few thousand dollars to start, that would work for Morgan as well. Buck was convinced and wrote Morgan a cheque for $6,000.

As the weeks went by, Morgan kept in constant contact with Buck, giving him updates on the petroleum project. The lawyer handling things in Nigeria was happy to provide Morgan and Buck with any documentation they needed. As the weeks turned to months, Morgan showed Buck the e-mails and the new certificates. Buck was convinced to put in more money, but only in small amounts of $4,000 to $6,000 at a time. Without realizing it, Buck had given Morgan almost $125,000 within eighteen months, in addition to the $50,000 for the real estate deal that still was waiting for home buyers.

At this time, Buck began to question Morgan more, and wanted to start getting some return on his investment. Morgan assured him that things were progressing as fast as they could, but deals of this magnitude take time. Moreover, the Nigerian government had so many barriers to releasing money out of the country.

As Buck became more insistent, Morgan told him that the money was available. He could probably arrange for Buck to get about $300,000 cash if he had another $10,000 available. If Buck was willing to fly to Nigeria and meet the lawyer acting for him, he could show him the cash and settle Buck's fears. Morgan even suggested that his wife accompany Buck to give him some company and to prove things were legitimate.

Buck and Morgan's wife, Delores, flew to Lagos, Nigeria, and contacted the lawyer, Midè Ogobuny, who agreed to meet them the following night. At the scheduled rendezvous, Buck and Delores showed up, and there was Midè and two other men standing beside an older Renault. Midè told Buck and Delores that the cash was in the trunk of the car and opened the hood. Inside the trunk was a case containing bundles of paper, about the size of United States or Canadian paper currency. But these bundles were all black.

Midè explained that these bills were treated with a special chemical to camouflage their appearance. Taking one of the notes from a stack, Midè produced a small plastic container and poured it over the note. The note began to change and revealed it to be a United States $100 bill.

According to Midè, the restrictions that the government placed on exporting currency out of the country made it difficult to move large amounts of cash easily. In order to move such large amounts, partners of Midè, who were chemists, developed a coating that would turn paper currency black. The money could then be shipped out of the country without detection by the authorities. Once the package of bills was received, a reversing agent then treated them and the money was ready to be deposited into a bank. The case in the trunk of the Renault held $5 million of treated money. If Buck was willing, he could transport it back to Canada. Midè would provide him with the chemicals needed to treat the notes once they were secure and out of the country.

It was like being in a spy novel to Buck. Everything was just as Morgan told him it was, and he saw it with his own eyes. Buck resolved to give Morgan the additional money when he returned to Canada and to make arrangements for the $5 million to be shipped to Canada.

Meanwhile, Morgan was also involved in other ventures that Buck was unaware of. Several years ago, Morgan had a small business providing water coolers to companies. The contracts were small, but lucrative, and had the potential for growth.

Morgan had approached his golfing partner, Alex, with a business proposal. He had just signed two large corporations to a contract for sixty months to provide them with water coolers. Morgan produced the contract with the signatures and showed the profit margin to Alex. If Alex would invest in the company, Cooling Spring Waters Inc., then Morgan would be able to expand the business.

The contract looked good to Alex, and he agreed to invest $100,000, writing Morgan four cheques of $25,000 each. Morgan then went looking for other investors and approached some members of his church, obtaining $340,000 from members of the congregation. He even obtained $60,000 from his daughter's new in-laws after showing them the signed contracts. In all, Morgan obtained $500,000 in investments for Cooling Spring Waters Inc.

Unknown to Morgan's investors, the original contracts that Morgan had with his clients had expired two years earlier. Most of the corporations had gone to contracted suppliers, purchased through their head offices. The contracts that Morgan showed to his investors were forged documents with new dates and signatures based on Morgan's original contracts.

In all business, there is a certain amount of trust expected between the parties. When the business proposition is between friends and family, that trust is implicit. However, certain precautions are still necessary to protect yourself and your friendship. In this case, going that extra step may have helped protect Morgan's victims. Asking for copies of recent paid invoices or purchase orders from both Morgan and his customers might have shown these victims something was not quite right with the deal.

Morgan was charged with fourteen counts of fraud and pled guilty to eight of them. He received a probationary sentence. The rest of the charges were withdrawn. He was also ordered to provide restitution to his victims. However, Morgan had declared bankruptcy and claimed he did not have any money to pay anyone. The church that he defrauded decided not to pursue any court action, either criminally or civilly, while one of the water cooler investors struck a secret deal with Morgan to get some of his money back before Morgan was charged.

In the end, the other victims joined together and sued Morgan in an effort to get their money back. After three years, the civil case has gone to court.

As for Buck and his investments, he lost all of the money he gave to Morgan. Morgan was never involved in land development nor was he connected to Pinnacle Land Development. Morgan had obtained at some time a prospectus from Pinnacle regarding their company and used this to create fake documents to show to potential investors.

Morgan did have connections in Lagos, Nigeria, but these connections were also part of the overall fraud scheme. Morgan was their "front-man" in Canada, and set up deals with victims whose trust he gained. Besides Buck, Morgan had convinced seven other victims to invest in the Nigerian Petroleum Company scheme. As a result, these victims sent over $600,000 to Nigeria and did not receive anything in return. To add insult to injury, Buck had paid for Morgan's wife to fly to Lagos to prove that the deal was legitimate.

THE PHARAOHS WEREN'T THE ONLY ONES TO BUILD PYRAMIDS

Christopher Malone was a salesman. It was what he had always wanted to do, and he knew he could do it well. Malone could talk to anyone and sell anything. He had been part of sales teams for furniture, automobiles, and electronics, and now he was selling shares in a very special organization.

The Canadian Adolescent Recovery and Support Network (CARSN) was setting up a system of recovery centres to help kids with drug problems. They would develop self-esteem, receive counselling, and still be able to attend school while recovering. The added bonus to investors was that by carefully and profitably investing funds, investors would be able to realize a return of 20 to 35 percent.

Using his connections in the retail trade and his wife's position on the Health Board, Malone went about selling shares to friends and colleagues. Investors would invest $10,000 and Malone would promise them a return within six months of 20 percent, or $2,000. The project had everything that an investor could want — a worthwhile charity that helped youth and a large return on an investment.

Malone was very busy contacting clients and obtaining their money for the CARSN program. Within six months, he was able to offer the promised return to his initial investors. But, as Malone explained, if these investors would keep the money with CARSN, their return would only increase. After seeing the first returns, these initial investors kept their money in the program. Malone kept selling investments and kept convincing the investors to let their money grow.

After eighteen months, some of the initial investors felt it was time to take their earnings and contacted Malone to give them their money. They would not be convinced to keep the money invested any longer; by their calculations, it should have almost doubled by now. Malone reluctantly paid his initial investors their money, but explained that due to the investment structure, the profits were not as high as he originally thought they would be. However, the rest of the money should be available in a week or so. The investors took the money offered and agreed to wait for the rest. Malone continued to sell investments, which he used to pay the investors their profits. However, the more investors who wanted their returns, the more Malone had to sell, until the scheme collapsed and Malone disappeared with $3 million.

This scheme is known as a Ponzi scheme, named after Charles Ponzi. Charles Ponzi was an Italian immigrant to the United States. In the 1920s, Ponzi convinced investors that he could take advantage of the difference between foreign and U.S. currencies used to purchase and sell international mail coupons. The basics of Ponzi's scheme were to purchase international mail coupons at a low price and then re-sell them at a higher price.

After the First World War, inflation in Italy had decreased the cost of postage. An agent could cheaply purchase an international mail coupon in U.S. funds and exchange it for U.S. stamps at a higher value. These U.S. stamps could then be sold for actual cash. Ponzi saw the potential profit in this and started his own company, the Securities Exchange Company, to manage the scheme. His initial startup cost was $30!

Ponzi offered his investors a 40 percent return on their investment. Initially, these investors were quickly paid their profits as promised. The word spread and more investors began pouring money into the scheme. Within seven months, Charles Ponzi was making millions. However, the entire scheme was hollow. None of the money that Ponzi collected was being re-invested into the company. An analysis at the time showed that over 160 million mail coupons would have to have been purchased by Ponzi, but there were less than 28,000 coupons in circulation. Yet, as long as the money kept coming in, Ponzi could pay investors and keep ahead of the eventual collapse.

When Ponzi's scheme collapsed, thousands of people lost their investments. His Securities Exchange Company was shut down, and Ponzi was indicted on eighty-six counts of fraud. Ponzi pled guilty to mail fraud and was sentenced to a total of fourteen years in prison. Federal officials tried to trace the money Ponzi obtained but were unable to do so. With his initial purchase of $30 to start his scheme, Charles Ponzi ended up stealing millions of dollars from investors.

The principle of the Ponzi scheme is one of "robbing Peter to pay Paul." As long as the scheme has a sufficient flow of money to complete the circle, it will continue. However, instead of a circle, the scheme tends to resemble a spiral. As the number of investors increase, the supply of new investors begins to decrease. The scheme collapses under its own weight.

Ponzi schemes resemble pyramid schemes as there is no real product being sold for the investment. A pyramid scheme, or multi-level sales program, gets its name from the pyramid structure of the organization. Usually there is a large sales base that pays royalties to a smaller, higher level, which in turn pays royalties to a still smaller, higher level, and so on to the top. As long as there is a product or service of real value being sold, and the salespersons receive money based on these sales, these pyramid organizations are legal.

However, if a person participating in the scheme receives a return on his or her investment for recruiting only, they are participating in an illegal pyramid scheme. The participants in these schemes are not offering a product for sale, the product has no value, or does not exist. Quite often the scheme is disguised in an elaborate set of investment rules that are poorly understood by the investors.

Related to pyramid schemes are chain letters. Chain letters again derive their name from the structure of the scheme, where each participant forms a link in the chain. A recipient of a chain letter will be promised something intangible, such as good luck, if they send the letter on to a number of friends, thereby keeping the chain going. Some chain letters tell how you can make money by recruiting several friends and sending cash back down the chain. These friends will then recruit more friends to send cash and you will eventually begin to get your portion. Once a chain letter asks you to send cash it becomes a pyramid scheme.

Under the Criminal Code of Canada and the Competition Act, all pyramid schemes and chain letters are illegal in Canada. Similar to pyramid and Ponzi schemes are lapping schemes. The difference is that lapping schemes are usually perpetrated against financial institutions.

SHE WAS MY FAVOURITE CUSTOMER?

Laura Sampson and her husband, Jason, owned a number of businesses in Winnipeg, Manitoba. The businesses were based on the copying and printing business. Laura looked after the finances of the companies, making deposits, paying bills, and so on, while Jason looked after the business itself. Business was good for the Sampsons. They vacationed in Hawaii, owned a large home in the western part of Winnipeg, and for Jason's birthday, Laura bought him a new Mustang convertible.

Laura continued to manage the finances and would go into the bank to make her deposits and transfers. She had struck up a friendship with a particular customer service representative named Shelly. If Shelly was busy, Laura was quite happy to wait until she was free.

What Shelly did not realize was that Laura was actually transferring funds among her three businesses, writing cheques for products and services that did not exist. For example, Laura would write a cheque from Company A for $15,000 and deposit it into the account of Company B. She would then write a cheque from Company B for $10,000 and deposit that cheque into the account for Company C. Laura would then write a cheque from Company C for $10,000 to Company A and deposit this into the account. This overlapping of cheques would show on the financial institution's books as Company A having a balance of $25,000, Company B a balance of $10,000, and Company C a balance of $10,000. The scheme relied on the delay that was incorporated into the bank's financial system for processing deposits and the willingness of the bank to carry the overdraft at least until the end of the business day.

Laura carried on this scheme until it was eventually caught by another customer service representative who was filling in for Shelly while she was on holidays. The unique aspect of Laura's scheme was that it was carried out entirely at the same branch. Usually a lapping scheme is carried out using several institutions and branches.

THE STRUCTURE OF PONZI AND PYRAMID SCHEMES

Most successful Ponzi and pyramid schemes share the same characteristics. First and foremost, they rely on the greed of the investors. The promise of substantial gain for little investment often overrides an investor's better judgment. Next, there is the promise that it is a surefire, guaranteed investment that cannot fail. If there are any doubts, the fraudster will offer to buy out the investor immediately, although this might result in a substantial transaction fee to the investor. Such an offer is not due to the benevolence of the fraudster, but in the hope that by buying out one dissatisfied investor, no one else will hear of problems and ask for their money as well.

Frequently the fraudster uses relatives, close friends, business associates, and acquaintances to get new victims. In Morgan's case, he was able to get $60,000 from his daughter-in-law's parents and $100,000 from his golfing partner. Once the investors realize that their money has gone, they often cling to the hope that somehow everything will work out in the end; either the investment will actually pay off, or the fraudster will do the right thing and pay back the money they took.

Finally, as with most fraud schemes, the fraudsters count on the victims being reluctant to admit to anyone, especially family members, that they have been cheated for the fear of looking greedy.

If you are approached, or are tempted to participate in what appears to be a Ponzi or pyramid scheme, there are a few things you should look for before you invest any money:

1. Beware of promises of high profits that are guaranteed a sure thing. Remember that nothing in life is guaranteed, least of all making money.
2. Avoid financial advisors who fail to provide clear explanations of the investment or use confusing jargon that makes them sound knowledgeable and you incompetent.

3. Ask for and obtain written details of the investment. Ask for bank statements, stock quotes, or statements from other investors. Be cautious of any details that cannot be verified in person.

4. Resist the pressure to reinvest without obtaining your profit first. If you do decide to invest, think about the investment as a day at the casino. Plan to invest or play with a certain amount. When you win or make that amount, pocket and continue to play with your "winnings."

Remember, if it seems too good to be true, it is. Also, remember that just as at the casino, the odds are always in favour of the house.

8

NIGERIAN/419 FRAUDS

In *The Speculations of Jefferson Thorpe*, Canadian author Stephen Leacock wrote of the misadventures of one Mr. Jefferson Thorpe of Mariposa, Ontario. Jefferson was a pillar of the community and owned the local barber shop: "A centre for gossip and profound thinking by the inhabitants of Mariposa." The inhabitants of Mariposa would come to Jefferson's shop to discuss and debate the issues of the day while having their hair cut or their beards shaved.

Jefferson takes his money, invests it all in the mining boom up North, and makes his fortune. Now well off, and respectable, Jefferson and his family are the toast of the town. It comes to pass that "some Cuban people" contact Jefferson, and they encourage him to invest in their proposition.

In describing the Cuban deal, Leacock explains, "These Cuban people wrote to Jeff from Cuba — or a post office box from New York — it's all the same thing because Cuba being so near to New York the mail is all distributed from there." They wanted Jefferson to invest in a land development in Cuba in plantations claimed from the insurrectos. How these investors heard of

Jefferson no one knew or cared to figure out, but they promised him a huge return for his investment, perhaps up to 400 percent.

The "Cuban gentlemen" go on to say, "They asked for no guarantee. Just send the money — whether by express order or bank draft or cheque, they left that to oneself, as a matter between Cuban gentlemen." Jefferson decides to invest in the deal and convinces other residents of Mariposa to invest as well. Of course, the Cuban land deal is a fraud and Jefferson loses his fortune. The other investors also lose their money, but life eventually returns to the way it was in Mariposa.[1]

This short story is part of Stephen Leacock's *Sunshine Sketches of a Small Town*, first published in 1912. The fraud Leacock describes has several elements that are still used today:

1. Unexpectedly contacted by someone from another country;
2. Using assets from a corrupt regime (the insurrectos);
3. The promise of a high return;
4. The use of a mailbox address; and
5. The trust that the fraudsters place in Jefferson to send the money without guarantees, "as a matter between Cuban gentlemen."

Sadly, some things never change.

MORE THAN JUST OIL CAN BE DIRTY

Philip was a successful and well-respected person in the oil industry in Calgary, Alberta, who lived in the affluent area of Mount Royal. He had built his company from nothing and was the epitome of the self-made man. He was educated and had written and published several books on the oil industry that were known to, and used by many in the oil patch.

As an oil executive and explorer, Philip had the opportunity to travel throughout the world and to meet many people from different cultures. After thirty years in the business, he was planning an active retirement, during which he would still dabble and speculate in the industry that made him a wealthy man.

One afternoon, Philip received a faxed letter from Nigeria written by a person claiming to be an associate in the oil industry who worked for the Nigerian National Petroleum Corporation. Philip had had dealings several years ago with the National Petroleum Company with their offshore oil wells, so he was not surprised to receive the letter.

From HARUNA ABUBAKAR

Dear Friend,

TRANSFER OF US$28.5M OVER INFLATED FUEL FUND

I am Alhaji Haruna Abubakar, former Director In-charge of Procurement and Purchases in the Petroleum Product Marketing Company (PPMC) a subsidiary of the Nigeria National Petroleum Corporation (NNPC). Now I'm a board member in NNPC During the military regime of General Sanni Abacha, our refineries were in bad condition and we were importing fuel.

Some top military officers and I collaborated and imported a low quality fuel at a reduced cost thereby inflating the purchasing cost to the tune of US$28.5 Million (Twenty Eight Million Five Hundred Thousand US Dollars) to help out ourselves during retirement. After the importation of the fuel and the death of Former Military Head of State of Nigeria, General Sanni Abacha, we could not process the claims and the voucher from the NNPC bank account immediately as all financial transactions to that effect was suspended by the subsequent regime.

We now, after duly completing all necessary banking pro!!ession wish to transfer the funds into a trusted account overseas. We wish to have this funds, which have lingered for long in the bank transferred overseas as soon as possible as there recent eyebrows being raised as regards the funds and further leaving the money in the bank here might jeopardize our claim to it. I write to solicit for your assistance in helping us provide a trusted bank account where tax will not take a large toll on the money as we have completed all necessary documentation to the release of this fund.

Requirements

1. Your company name and address, private phone and fax numbers.
2. Complete banking information, address with all necessary communication contacts.

My colleagues and I have agreed to give you 25% for accepting to secure this fund into your account and we have set aside 5% to cover upfront expenses. My colleagues and I will share the remaining 70%. I will furnish you with more details on your response.

Note as soon as we submit your details as the contractor, the bank will contact you henceforth and will see you as the true contractor and we cannot change that any more so we need your absolute confidence. We would do all these arrangements ourselves but we are being Watched by Government officials all of the Time. You may be required by the bank to pay certain little transfer charges for the transfer of the money, we do hope you shall consider all these before accepting to assist. This informs why we have given you the above (25%) percentage commision for your assistance and we shall also repay you for all expences incured from the 5% set aside for it.

Best regards,

Haruna Abubakar [*sic*]

Philip remembered his time in Africa speculating and dealing with various government agencies. This letter sounded reasonable because he knew that the various government officials there were corrupt, and bribing them was merely a matter of business. Philip contacted Abubakar and provided him with the information he requested, stating that he would be willing to be his partner in this endeavour.

Shortly thereafter, Philip received a letter in the mail postmarked Nigeria. Inside was a contract between himself, Abubakar, and his partners. The terms of the contract were as originally claimed in the fax that Philip had received. All that was needed to close the deal was for Philip to send him a cheque for $35,000 to cover some of the "little transfer charges," and as a show of good faith. Philip sent the cheque to the return address indicated in the contract and waited to hear from his new partners. To Philip, this was just like the old days when he was making and brokering deals and being a player in the field.

Two to three weeks later, Philip received another letter in the mail. Inside was a cheque for $168,000 and a covering letter. The letter explained that Philip was to deposit the cheque into his account. The letter went on to explain that $100,000 from the cheque was Philip's first return on his investment. Philip was also informed that Abubakar would need $50,000 for some more charges that came to light. The money was needed as soon as possible, so could Philip please take $50,000 from the cheque and wire the money directly to them? Abubakar told Philip that he could keep the balance of $18,000 for his inconvenience and trouble. In effect, Philip had made $118,000 in a few weeks.

Philip went to his bank and wired another $50,000 to his partners, and then deposited the cheque into his account. After five days, the bank notified Philip that the cheque he had deposited had been returned as a counterfeit cheque. Philip couldn't understand how this could happen. He went home, contacted his partners, and asked for an explanation.

Abubakar stated that he was shocked to learn the cheque was counterfeit because that was what the "little transfer charges" were for, to ensure the cheques were legitimate. In fact, Abubakar had given his contact $20,000 of his own money to ensure this would not happen. Abubakar ensured Philip that he would get to the bottom of this.

After a few more weeks, Philip received another letter from Abubakar, who stated that the contact was discovered murdered the day after he had given Abubakar the cheque. Nevertheless, Abubakar had another contact that could negotiate and provide the funds to Philip and him. Included with the letter was another cheque for $89,000 with a request that Philip deposit it and wire $40,000 to Abubakar. Philip was to keep the remaining $49,000 to reimburse him for the $50,000 he had sent earlier. Philip sent the money and deposited the cheque, but again the cheque was returned to the bank as counterfeit.

This pattern continued with Philip and Abubakar for several months. Philip also began to get offers and proposals from other parties. The last time Philip tried to deposit and cash a cheque, he was arrested for uttering a forged document. He also had on him, at the time of his arrest, fourteen other cheques in various amounts adding up to $358,500. When questioned by the police, Philip estimated he had invested over $900,000 in the Nigerian National Petroleum Corporation, and he has not wavered in his belief that this is just a matter of doing business and that he will be amply compensated for his trouble.

The original letter that Philip received is commonly referred to as a Nigerian Letter or 419 letter, 419 being the Nigerian Criminal Code section for fraud. Philip's letter is by far the most common format and it is difficult to find someone who has not received or seen one of these appeals. Nigerian letters do not always have to describe a business deal. Some appeal for donations for disaster relief, some offer to purchase items you may have listed on the Internet, while others may take on a style like the following:

> Good day Sir:
> My name is Master Corporal Terry Parson, 101st U.S. Rangers. I am currently posted to Iraq as part of the operation to locate Osama Bin Laden. While leading my Section through one of the remote villages our rockets uncovered a hidden tunnel and escape route. Inside was a safe containing a small amount of jewels and $15 million in U.S. currency.

This money was probably acquired through criminal means and used to finance terrorist attacks against Americans. By the rules of engagement I am required to turn over any found money to my superiors so that it can be redistributed to officials in this country.

As a Christian, I believe that it is wrong to turn over this money to the same people that we are fighting.

I am looking for someone, and I hope that it is you, that is willing to be a partner in sharing this wealth. I propose that I send you the money and that you deposit it into your bank account, or invest it. I will send the cash in several packages to your attention. With this money back home in the United States we can put it to better use than returning it to another corrupt regime.

I have made the initial inquiries and I will need a cheque or money order from you in the amount of $10,000 USD to cover the shipping and quiet any customs personnel here. If you are the person that I pray you are let me know as soon as possible. Keeping this amount of cash a secret is difficult to do under these circumstances.

God Bless America

These Nigerian letters often have several common characteristics that should be noted by anyone receiving them. They are rarely addressed to a specific person, unless the fraudster used a name database or mooch list. Instead, they are addressed to "My Dear Friend" or like these letters, "Dear Friend" or "Good Day Sir." The sentence structure is often broken with little or incorrect punctuation and overly long sentences, and the spelling is often very poor.

Other characteristics include:

- Capital letters that are used to emphasize a point, especially the money being offered.
- The sender is often a professional person, doctor, lawyer, or

high-ranking official.

- The receiver's trust is often questioned, putting him or her on the defensive.
- The offer is always limited before it goes to another prospective investor. The offer always shows how the proceeds will be fairly divided, and will require your banking information, a cheque, or a money order to complete the deal.
- Finally, the whole deal generally centres on the fraudsters having committed an illegal or immoral act, such as stealing money from their corrupt government or smuggling jewels and converting them to cash. The fraudsters then ask you to become party to that act by helping them launder their money through your bank account. This, of course, happens only if any money is actually sent.

It's almost impossible to get your money back if you have already sent it off. Going to the country concerned is not recommended, as you run the very real risk of becoming injured or killed. These people are criminals, not legitimate business people who made a mistake. Playing games with these criminals, such as leading them on with promises of your own, or imposing conditions, is not advisable either. Although you may get a sense of personal satisfaction by pretending to have been duped and stringing them along, you do run the risk of retaliation.

If you receive a fax, letter, or e-mail, here are some suggestions to limit your risk:

- Don't transact business with an unfamiliar person.
- Always ask for and verify the documentation you receive.
- Do a background check on your business partner.
- Ask yourself, can I get my money back if it fails?
- Never pay fees for uninitiated services.
- Don't be pressured or hurried into making decisions.
- If you decide to respond, limit your financial risk.
- Be sure that the amount you're giving would not greatly jeopardize your finances, should you lose the money.

9

CREDIT CARD SCAMS

DID I ORDER THAT?

Maryanne lived in Phoenix, Arizona, and had a lot of friends who would come from Canada in the winter to enjoy the warmth and sunshine that Arizona has to offer. Maryanne required several prescription drugs, and through these friends she learned that she could purchase cheaper drugs from Canada than the United States.

Maryanne located and contacted a prescription company in Regina, Saskatchewan, called International Care Pharmacy Distributors. International Care Pharmacy Distributors was a respectable company that offered prescriptions to American clients at a rate much less than they would have to pay at home. Because of the savings and the convenience of having her prescriptions shipped directly to her, Maryanne became a client.

Maryanne registered with International Care and provided her mailing address, phone number, credit card information, and everything else that was necessary for her to do business with the company. Maryanne became a satisfied customer for over eighteen months without any incident or problem. She would call when her prescription was running low, and the company would fill her order and ship it to her that same day.

On one occasion in July, Maryanne called and renewed her prescription with Rachel, a customer service agent with International Care. The order was for $135 for one prescription and $123 for a second, totaling $258. Rachel processed the order and the prescription was filled and sent that same day. In August, Maryanne received her credit card statement and paid the outstanding balance of $785. At first, Maryanne did not think that this was out of the ordinary because she had made some purchases for her granddaughter's birthday a couple of weeks before. However, subconsciously, the amount of the statement didn't seem right to her.

A week after paying the credit card bill, Maryanne looked at the bill again and discovered that there was a charge on her credit card from International Care Pharmacy Distributors, for a second amount of $258. There was also a processing fee from Western Union for the purchase of a money gram to Regina of $35. Maryanne contacted Western Union, who explained that International Care Pharmacy Distributors in Regina had requested the money gram. Western Union provided all of the information regarding the money gram including the date, wire number, and the location that it was cashed. With this information, Maryanne contacted her local police department, which in turn contacted the Saskatoon Police for investigation.

International Care Pharmacy Distributors was shocked that one of their customer service people abused the confidentiality of their clients, and they cooperated fully with the investigation. By tracing the prescription orders, they learned that the customer service agent who had filled Maryanne's prescription was Rachel Billings. Rachel had been an employee of International Care Pharmacy Distributors for two years. She was in her late forties and had been divorced for almost ten years. Rachel did not have many friends at International Care because she had a bullying nature that made people avoid her when they could. In fact, there had been complaints about her behaviour in the last few months, which the manager of International Care had yet to address.

Rachel also liked to play bingo. She could be found at the bingo hall nearly every night of the week. Rachel had used the opportunity of Maryanne's order to submit a charge for a duplicate amount on Maryanne's credit card.

When International Care Pharmacy Distributors looked into Rachel's activities more thoroughly, they learned that she had done this to several of their clients. The amounts generally were between $75 and $125 dollars, but were always duplicates of the client's purchase. This amount, Rachel believed, would be dismissed as what it appeared to be, a second charge for prescriptions that the client ordered. Usually, by the time the credit card statement arrived, the client would not remember that they had not ordered or received a second prescription. Through this scheme, Rachel collected $15,000 in under eighteen months. It was only when she attempted to charge Maryanne for a larger amount that she was caught.

The Regina Police tracked the money gram to the Western Union location where Rachel had cashed it, and were able to obtain witnesses who identified her. Rachel was charged with this offence and pled guilty, receiving a six-month probationary sentence. International Care Pharmacy Distributors reimbursed Maryanne for the extra charges and implemented better controls within their company.

WHEN HOSTELS BECOME HOSTILE

The Western Canadian Institute of Applied Science and Technology (WCIAST) of Saskatoon, Saskatchewan, is a world-renowned technical institute. It attracts students and lecturers from across Canada and around the world. Like most colleges and universities, the facility houses students attending classes from around the world, as well as allowing guest lecturers to avail themselves of accommodations on the campus.

Dirk was one of these guest lecturers who stayed at the WCIAST residence for the month of July, while he was teaching and doing research. When he checked out of the residence, he paid for his room with his credit card and obtained copies of his receipt. When Dirk returned home to Germany, he received an invoice in November from his credit card with three charges that he did not make. In addition to his residence fees, two additional charges were credited to WCIAST and one to a local cable television provider. The amounts charged to Dirk's card were over $1,200.

WCIAST rents out their residences during the summer when there are no classes running and the majority of the students are away. These rates are much lower than a regular hotel rate and are taken advantage of by a number of students and travellers on a budget. Mary, who lives in New Zealand but has family living in Saskatoon, decided to travel to Saskatoon to attend her niece's wedding. Mary decided to take advantage of the low rates offered at WCIAST and stay at the residence, also paying for her room with her credit card. After Mary returned home that November, she received an invoice for an additional $420 that she had not authorized.

When the police were called in to investigate these suspicious transactions, shift schedules and transaction records were reviewed. In addition, the cable television provider was served a production order to obtain the client information for the bill that Dirk's credit card paid for. After the records were examined, the police learned that there were four other suspicious transactions made between July and November of that same year.

Jordan was a student studying at WCIAST on an international student visa. He lived in the residence and always paid cash for his room at the end of each month. In July, Jordan made his regular cash payment towards his residence bill. When the police examined this transaction, the record showed that a correction was made to the account, cancelling the cash payment, and that $3,500 was charged to a credit card holder who lived in California.

In October, another student, Callista, also made two cash payments towards her residence bill. These two payments, totaling $1,600, also showed corrections made to the account, cancelling the cash payments and charging the amount to another cardholder in Tokyo. This happened with other students, including Oludele, whose payment was charged to Dirk's card, and Paul, whose payment was charged to Mary's.

The police investigation showed that although the cash payments were accepted by different staff members of the residence, all of the corrections and subsequent billings were made by one staff member. As well, the cable television bill, which was paid by Dirk's credit card, was traced to that same employee. The employee confessed to committing these and other frauds. He had obtained over $20,000 in six months, charging the amounts to victims and international students from around the world. As a result, he was charged with six counts of fraud. Because the victims were from out of the country, a deal was struck where he pled guilty to two of the charges for which he would receive one year probation, while the other four charges were withdrawn.

For the majority of people, credit card and bank card statements are another record of our expenses. We tend to ignore them. We pay the minimum amount and continue our spending habits without really checking our statements. If we do check our statements, the various codes and fees are so foreign to us that we simply accept them as legitimate. Fraudsters rely on this complacency to achieve their goal. How many of us have ignored or even noticed that $5 service charge per month, or the $1.25 transaction fee from an ATM?

One woman unknowingly paid $25 a month for unemployment insurance on her credit card, in case she was out of work and couldn't pay her bills. However, she was self-employed and had no need of the insurance. She didn't become aware of the extra billing until her boyfriend noticed it. By then she had paid over $1,000 for an unnecessary expense. Although a legitimate business was charging her this amount, the fraud principle is still the same. Small amounts are often ignored and paid without question.

10

FRAUDS COMMITTED BY FRIENDS AND FAMILY

The following examples of frauds make up the large majority of fraud investigators' case loads. They are usually for relatively small amounts and are carried out against friends, acquaintances, or family members. Although the dollar amount may be small, the impact for these victims may be just as traumatic as a multi-thousand dollar fraud against a company or someone else. The loss of trust and the feelings of embarrassment are arguably worse when the fraud is committed by a friend or family member. Investigators and the courts should always consider the effect that a fraud has on a victim, no matter the amount of the loss.

WHAT ARE FRIENDS FOR?

Jason and his girlfriend, Alexis, were at Chinook Centre in Calgary, Alberta, doing some shopping before their university term ended. Charlie, an old friend of Jason's, approached him and asked if Jason could cash a cheque for him. Jason had played football with Charlie about five years earlier and had not seen him since the end of that season.

Charlie explained to Jason that he had just received his paycheque and didn't have a chance to cash it before the bank had closed. Now that it was the weekend, he was stuck without any cash to pay a cab to get home. Charlie was hoping Jason could deposit the cheque into his account and then withdraw it again and give him the cash. For doing him this favour, Charlie would give Jason $40 so he and his girlfriend could have lunch as Charlie's treat. Jason wanted to help him out. He knew what it was like to be short of cash, especially on a Saturday night. Jason deposited the $400 cheque through the ATM and then withdrew it, giving Charlie $360. The other $40 Charlie told him to keep.

On Monday, Jason went to the ATM and tried to withdraw $20 for lunch at university. The ATM showed insufficient funds. Jason couldn't understand. There should have been $200 in his account. Charlie's cheque turned out to be NSF, and Jason was on the hook to the bank for the $400.

This is a common scheme that is revived every few years. It generally affects younger people, because they are more trusting and willing to take a person's word. The fraudster's excuses range from not having a bank card, the cheque is from babysitting, or another friend gave them the cheque. Unfortunately, the person who cashes the cheque is responsible to the bank for the funds. The easiest way to combat this type of fraud is to not cash cheques for anyone unless you know him or her very well.

In the case of Charlie and Jason, Charlie tricked Jason into cashing his cheque because he took advantage of their acquaintance. Charlie was eventually charged with the criminal act of fraud. Jason could apply through the courts for restitution of his money; however, the amount of money was not worth the inconvenience or time it would have cost him. It should be noted that when a court orders a fraudster to pay restitution, it is often up to the victim to collect the money owed to them. In numerous cases, if the fraudster fails to pay, the victim will then have to resort to a civil suit, even though the fraudster was convicted, to recover their money.

WATER IS THICKER THAN BLOOD

Dannie was a hard man. He worked hard, he lived hard, and he drank hard. He lived on a ranch in the Nicola Valley of British Columbia, where he ranched for most of his life. When his wife died, he met Susan, who was just as hard as Dannie. This was probably just as well, as no one else would have been able to live with Dannie all of those years.

Dannie sold his farm when it was becoming too much work for him to manage, but he still lived on the homestead. He had a modest pension from the sale, which, combined with his government pension, kept Susan and him doing alright.

It was at the homestead that Dannie suffered his first stroke. It seemed like all of those years of hard living had finally caught up to him. Dannie was unable to speak or write, but he could move his head slightly in response to some questions. Dannie was moved into a care facility where he could receive the full time care that Susan was not able to provide. The money from the sale of the ranch would look after the expenses and the pension would pay any other bills.

Dannie had three children, who had all moved away. Richard and Gloria had moved to Victoria and had been in a bit of trouble with the law a few years back, and Simon was a realtor living in Kelowna. Simon would visit Dannie more often than his brother and sister because it was closer for him to drive. None of the children would visit, however, if Susan was there. They felt, rightly or wrongly, that she was the cause of all of Dannie's problems.

After eighteen months, Susan received a notice in the mail from the care facility, stating that the bill for Dannie's care had not been paid for over a year. Susan was perplexed; she had set up automatic deductions from Dannie's bank account.

It so happened that while on one of his visits, Simon had brought along an old family friend. Dannie had been able to recognize Michael, a realtor and a commissioner for oaths in British Columbia. Simon had contacted him a couple of weeks earlier and told him how Susan was taking advantage of Dannie's infirmity to skim off money for her drinking and gambling. Simon wanted to protect Dannie by obtaining power of attorney and controlling any of his funds.

Michael drafted the papers and went to the hospital with Simon. Simon spoke to Dannie and told him what Susan was doing and asked if Dannie wanted Simon to have power of attorney. Dannie made a movement with his head, which Simon interpreted as a yes and convinced Michael that this was what Dannie wanted. Simon then held Dannie's hand and helped him to sign his name on the papers transferring power of attorney. Michael signed as a witness and was able to get one of the nurses at the facility to sign as a witness as well.

Simon then went to Dannie's bank and had all funds redirected to his bank in Kelowna, so that he could control the funds. Another realtor also signed the transfer forms as a witness at Dannie's request, even though she had not been at the hospital. But Simon was her friend and she wanted to help him out.

Unknown to everyone, Simon had a cocaine addiction that cost him hundreds of dollars a day. He had lost his job and his realtor licence and was doing anything to support his habit. The police had questioned him regarding his involvement in a murder of a local drug dealer but were unable to obtain sufficient evidence for an arrest. Simon had used the power of attorney to access Dannie's money and support his cocaine habit.

It is a strange reality that families who have been close and harmonious will often change and become bitter rivals and enemies upon the death of a parent; especially when there is some form of inheritance involved. One side will often believe that they deserve a larger share, because of the attention or care that they have provided, or whatever reason makes sense to them.

We all believe that we can trust family to do what is right and fair, no matter what the circumstances. But who determines what is right and fair? The best way to stop problems before they happen is for the parent to have their affairs in order with the use of a lawyer, financial investor, or financial planner. These professionals have the necessary knowledge and expertise to help make the best decisions. They are also detached from the family, and work only in the interest of their client to meet their needs.

The end result in the case involving Dannie and his family was that Simon was charged with fraud. He had left the province and an arrest warrant was issued for him. Richard and Gloria, Dannie's other son and daughter, helped Susan pay the money owed for Dannie's care. Meanwhile, no charges were filed against Michael, who had acted as the commissioner for oaths, or the other realtor who signed as a witness because there was insufficient evidence to support a charge. Michael still has a thriving real estate business in British Columbia.

MOTHER ISN'T ALWAYS RIGHT

Kim had moved out of her parents' home two years ago. She had not been able to get along with her mother for a long time before that, and had finally made the decision to move on. Kim moved into a small apartment and purchased a modest amount of furniture and a used car. In March, Kim applied for a store credit card in order to purchase a new television. Kim was shocked to find that her credit application was turned down, and that she owed $7,500 on her credit cards. This was all news to Kim, as she had never applied for a credit card until that day.

Kim contacted the credit company and learned that she had apparently applied for a credit card over two years ago, and that a second card was added to the application in her mother's name. Kim was sent a record of the purchases, which showed purchases of fuel, groceries, and liquor, all made within blocks of Kim's old address, where her mother still lived.

All of the bills had been sent to the same address, but none of them had been paid. The matter was now in collection.

I WANT TO BE JUST LIKE MY SISTER

In October, Audra's telephone service and her gas service were cut off. When Audra made inquiries as to why, she was told that she had not paid her bills for over four months and had ignored all attempts by the companies involved to contact them and rectify the problem.

Audra was surprised to learn that she had such an outstanding debt because she had always paid her bills on time. When she looked into the matter further, she learned that although the telephone and gas service was being provided to her house, the billing address was to her sister's residence in Brandon, Manitoba.

Audra contacted the RCMP, which began investigating and learned that Audra's sister, Corrine, had applied for gas service to her own residence in Audra's name for billing purposes. Corrine had also applied for, and opened, seven accounts for cell phone service, again in Audra's name. Additionally, Corrine had applied online for a credit card in Audra's name, providing all of the correct information required, including identification, which Corrine had stolen during one of her infrequent visits to Audra's home. Using this credit card, Corrine made several purchases through the Internet and had them delivered to her home in Brandon.

IF YOU CAN'T TRUST YOUR BOYFRIEND ...

Lynda was living with her common-law husband, Keith. In May, Keith applied for a MasterCard in his name with a second card to be issued to Lynda. Lynda did not know of this application or of her having a card issued to her. Keith had intercepted the mail and had kept Lynda's card hidden in his dresser drawer.

Keith would use his MasterCard and make the payments without incident. However, for several reasons, things were not working out between Keith and Lynda. In the spring, Keith moved out. In the fall of that year, Lynda received a letter from Financial Recovery Systems, acting as an agent for the bank, claiming she owed $7,000.

Lynda contacted the police and copies of the original MasterCard application were obtained from the bank. Lynda recognized the handwriting on the application form as her ex-common-law husband, Keith. Lynda provided copies of her signature to the police and completed an affidavit stating that she had no knowledge of the credit card application. An affidavit, or statutory declaration, is a sworn, legal document. It briefly states that the facts you are stating are true and that you swear to the information provided under oath. Often, the police or financial investigators will require that you swear to an affidavit before they begin an investigation. Swearing to a false affidavit is a criminal offence.

As the police looked into the transactions for the account, they learned that for two years until that spring, all of the card transactions were made with Keith's card. However, after he moved out, the purchases began with the card issued to Lynda.

Lynda had no idea where Keith had gone and the police applied for an arrest warrant. The bank accepted Lynda's affidavit and did not hold her responsible for the credit card charges.

... WHO CAN YOU TRUST?

Mira had been going to college during the day in order to upgrade her skills and obtain better employment. She had two children and lived with her boyfriend, Emmanuel. She had known Emmanuel for at least four years and had lived with him for one year. One day, Mira's bank contacted her and informed her of several fraudulent transactions on her account. The bank also told her that surveillance photos had been ordered and that she should report the matter to the police.

When the police obtained the photos, they were shown to Mira, who immediately identified the person as her boyfriend. Emmanuel had obtained her bank card and had withdrawn $500 from her account without her knowledge. He was arrested and charged with theft of Mira's bank card and fraud. He pled guilty to the fraud charge and the theft of the card was withdrawn. Emmanuel received a six-month probationary sentence. Mira had Emmanuel move out. She completed her college diploma and is now a counsellor for abused women.

•   •   •

Sometimes you cannot stop yourself from being a victim, as in Kim, Lynda, Mira, and Audra's cases. Members of their family, people they would have never suspected, had deceived all four. In cases such as these, the victim has two choices: absorb the loss and move on, or confront the family member and report the fraud to the credit company and to the police. Most credit card companies will require a police report or case number before they will consider clearing you of the debt. A police report shows them that your claim is more likely to be legitimate, rather than an attempt to avoid paying your bills.

Lynda, Audra, and Kim were eventually exonerated. In Audra's case, her telephone and gas service were restored, though her family went without these services for over a week. It took over six months to restore Audra's credit and to stop the phone calls and letters from collection agencies. In Lynda and Kim's cases, no charges were laid against the offenders due to insufficient evidence. The original application forms that Keith and Kim's mother had completed had been destroyed by the credit card company and replaced with a digital copy, which was inadmissible as evidence. The handwriting on these forms was also inadmissible because they were not from original documents that could be produced in court. As a result, the crown's office determined that there was not a likelihood of a conviction and the charges were not laid.

11

IDENTITY THEFT

NO DOWN PAYMENT, A LIFETIME OF PAYING

David and his friend Jeff drove into Saint John from Moncton, New Brunswick, for a company hockey tournament. The two friends had worked for a local car dealership and the dealers had started an amateur league in the Maritime Provinces for their employees. The games would be played over two days, which left David and Jeff time to go shopping for home electronics. Jeff was interested in buying a new stereo system for his apartment so this was a good opportunity to see what was available in a different city.

Jeff and David walked into the store and were met by Tyson Wright, the assistant sales manager for Sound Happenings, a province-wide stereo chain that specialized in high-end quality electronics. Jeff told Wright what he was looking for and Wright knew exactly what Jeff needed.

The store had just received the latest home-theatre package with digital programming that could be integrated into your computer, DVD recording, MP3 capability, and much more. The store listed the system at

$15,345. Wright was a hockey fan and showed a great deal of interest in the tournament. Wright also knew that as a young man, money is always tight and obtaining credit for big ticket items was often difficult, even if you had a steady job as Jeff had. Considering he had done well on his sales that month, Wright told Jeff that he could mark the price down to $7,500, but Jeff had to make up his mind today.

Jeff knew that this was the system that he wanted but was not ready to spend $7,500 on it at that time. They were in town for the tournament and had to be back at the arena within the hour. Wright understood completely, but he also knew that he could not keep this deal forever. What he would do is write up a provisional sales agreement. As Wright explained to David and Jeff, it was similar to applying for credit with the store. It would also help to establish a credit rating for Jeff for future purchases, like a car or a house. Having the agreement in place would allow Wright to explain to his boss that the system was on hold for this great price. Wright would hold onto the application forms and if Jeff could not make it back by closing, he would shred the forms.

This looked like the ideal solution. Jeff agreed to complete the forms. He gave Wright his driver's license and a credit card to copy for the application and filled in his personal information. David was convinced to complete an agreement as well in case he wanted a system in the future. That way, according to Wright, David would be pre-approved and would not have to go through the hassle of applying again.

David and Jeff left the store and went back to the tournament. They won their game but lost the next, coming in fourth in the dealership league. By the time the games were over, it was too late to go back to the store. They forgot about the stereo and returned to Moncton.

Eight months later, Jeff received a notice in the mail from a credit company telling him that he had missed his payments and that he owed $7,500. Jeff called the company to find out what was going on, and was told that he had purchased a stereo system from Sound Happenings and he owed them the money. Jeff explained that he did not purchase the stereo, but the credit company was insistent. Jeff was told that if he did not start making payments, his credit rating would be destroyed and legal action would take place. Jeff told the company to go ahead and hung up the phone. Meanwhile, David received the same letter in his mail.

Wright had been working a scheme for several months at the Sound Happenings store. He would spot potential customers and would convince them to complete a sales agreement. The agreement was actually a credit application that went through a credit/finance company. Wright would fax the completed application to a contact at the credit company, and the application would be approved for the amount of the purchase. Wright would also arrange for a six-month no payment option. In this way, the victims would not be aware of the scheme for several months. Wright also had partners working the same scheme in some of the other stores in New Brunswick.

Three months after hanging up on the credit company, Jeff applied for a car loan at the bank he had been dealing with for five years and where his pay cheque was deposited. According to the bank's credit rating, Jeff had a negative rating and the bank would not approve the loan. David moved into a new apartment and applied for telephone service and was told he was not approved for service due to his credit rating. It would take over two years for David, Jeff, and other victims of this scheme to have their credit rating restored.

As it turned out, Wright committed this fraud against thirty-five victims over an eight-month period. When a potential customer entered the store, they would be approached to purchase some merchandise. In order to complete the deal, the customer would be urged to complete an application for credit, allegedly to hold the price of the product. Once the customer left the store, the credit application would be put through as a "ghost deal." A ghost deal is a sale using either a non-existent person, or a person who has entered the store and provided credit information but has not purchased any merchandise. This person would then receive an invoice in the mail several months later requesting payment for this purchase.

In several instances, certain information would be altered on the original application form, and then it would be submitted to the contract credit company for approval. In some occurrences, the sales representative would have a contact at the credit company's local office, which would approve the application and, in some cases, increase the credit limit.

Once approved, the sales representative would process the ghost deal and remove the merchandise from the store. In addition, the fraudster would also claim the commission for the sale from the company. To make this scheme work better, Wright would pay the store administrators cash to ignore the transactions and the merchandise leaving the store. Wright would take the merchandise from the store after closing and take it to a friend's house. From there, he would sell it to other friends and acquaintances or sell it from the trunk of his car. On one occasion, Wright sold a home theatre system, valued in the store at $12,000, to the owner of a car dealership for $5,000.

Sometimes, Wright, or others from the store involved in this scheme, would simply take the merchandise to a pawn shop. Although the pawn shop would have records of who sold them the merchandise, there was little the police could do to recover the store's property. Sound Happenings had the make and model numbers of the equipment, but they did not have serial numbers to positively identify it. As well, internal sales incentives, where salespersons could receive merchandise for exceptional performance, also clouded the issue of what was stolen and what was given away.

In the end, Wright and five other employees were fired and charged with forty-eight counts of fraud. Sound Happenings estimated that it had lost over $2 million in sales and lost merchandise in three months. None of the stolen merchandise was ever recovered and returned to the store. To date, none of the culprits have appeared in court to face the charges.

As a twist to the story, all of the employees fired from the store made an application to the labour relations board for wrongful dismissal and for their vacation pay and commission pay. The board sided with the employees and ordered the store to pay all money owed.

Ignoring calls from credit companies and hanging up the telephone is one sure way to create problems for yourself. If you are a victim of fraud or identity theft, the sooner you acknowledge the fact and work with the police and credit companies, the sooner your credit issues can be resolved.

By failing to monitor their sales staff, Sound Happenings allowed Wright and the other employees to take advantage of them. Without properly recording their inventory by verifying what is sold and documenting serial numbers, Sound Happenings was unable to recover any of its merchandise. Believing that the property is yours is one thing, proving that it is yours is another. Sound Happenings closed all of their stores throughout the Maritimes and filed for bankruptcy.

A HIKE IN THE WOODS CAN CHANGE YOU ... LITERALLY

Carmen Simons was an enthusiastic backpacker. Any opportunity would find him out in the woods on a day hike either alone or with friends. It was on such a trip that Carmen became a victim of identity theft.

Carmen had planned for an eight-hour hike in the Gatineau Mountains. He had his pack and supplies, including emergency equipment in case he had to stay out for the night. He headed into the park on a Friday morning. Carmen had decided to lock his wallet, personal digital assistant (PDA), and a change of clothes in the trunk of his car while he was out. When Carmen returned to his car after the day's hike, he discovered that the driver-side window had been smashed and the contents of the trunk had been taken. Carmen drove home and reported the theft to the police.

Danny was a petty criminal who had been in and out of jail all of his life. His specialty was breaking into houses and stealing electronics — televisions, stereos, computers, or anything else that would get him a few dollars. He was not sophisticated, but he managed to get by. This afternoon he was going to meet an associate downtown to sell him a couple of pieces that he got the day before. Danny was always looking to make a quick buck or two.

When Danny met Mike, he told him that yesterday he had been in the Gatineau Park and had broken into a number of cars parked in the lot. From them he was able to get quite a few wallets and a PDA. Danny kept the cash but wanted to know if Mike wanted to buy the identification and the PDA. Mike knew the types of scams that this kind of identification would allow him to pull off, so he agreed, giving Danny

$100 for all of the identification, including the wallet and PDA belonging to Carmen. Taking Carmen's Social Insurance card and a couple other cards from his wallet, Mike went to a branch of Carmen's bank and posed as Carmen Simons. Mike told the Customer Service Representative that he wanted to open an account at that bank because he was in this area of town a lot. He produced his identification and arranged for Carmen's account to be closed and the money to be transferred from Carmen's other bank into his account. By using Carmen's Social Insurance card and other identification, the bank teller did not feel the need to ask for picture identification. There weren't any alerts posted on the account so the bank arranged for the transfer. Mike also obtained a new bank card to make withdrawals from the account.

On Monday morning, Carmen contacted his bank to start the process of getting new cards. When the manager checked, she informed him that his account had been closed and his money was transferred to another bank. Carmen no longer had an account or money at that bank.

The term "identity theft" has become more prevalent, meaning everything from debit and credit card skimming to taking over a person's identity. Often this generic term is misleading, but it does serve to categorize this type of fraud.

Often, victims of identity theft do not realize that they have been victimized until it is too late to stop it. Fraudsters are able to obtain information in a variety of ways. Some, like in Carmen's case, will steal wallets or purses from cars or office buildings. Others will steal mail from outside mailboxes. It is interesting to note that once mail is delivered in Canada, it is no longer the responsibility of Canada Post. Any such theft becomes a theft of property, not a theft of mail.

Other fraudsters will dig through trash (or what is referred to as "dumpster diving") to obtain forms, applications, and billing records that the fraudster can use to set up a new account or take over the services provided. Still others obtain the information in more complex ways, posing as someone who has a legitimate need of the information such as a census taker.

With the advent of the Internet, a new method of obtaining information has developed termed phishing or spoofing. Phishing is the method by which a fraudster spams the Internet claiming to be a legitimate company, often a financial institution. Generally, there will be a message claiming that activity was noticed on your account or that security upgrades are being performed. You will be instructed to click on the link to access the website. Once you click on the site, you are directed to a website that looks like a legitimate website for the company. Dialogue boxes appear that prompt you to provide your personal information to verify the company's records. Sometimes credit card numbers are also collected. You are then politely thanked and informed that if there are any further problems, you will be contacted.

Regardless of how the fraudster obtains an identity, it is what is done with it that can create major concerns. In Carmen's case, the information was used on a local level to open an account and obtain money and credit. In other cases, the information is sold or traded to others who manufacture new identities and new credit cards in cities and countries nowhere near where you live.

If you lose your identity, driver's licence, credit card, etc., it is imperative that you report the loss as soon as you are able. The sooner it's reported, the less you may be held responsible for by the credit card company. Most financial institutions would rather customers report their cards lost or stolen, even if they are simply misplaced, than run the risk of fraudsters using them.

Credit card and debit card skimming are also a growing method of obtaining your information. Skimming operations can take several forms, but all strive to obtain the same end result. The owner swipes the card to complete a transaction, the code is entered, and the transaction is completed. However, there are numerous ways to intercept the information and provide it to the fraudster.

Traditionally, there were two methods of surreptitiously obtaining card information. The first would involve a fake terminal where the owner of the card would swipe the card in what he believes to be a legitimate terminal. A fraudster would construct a fake pin-pad terminal that is identical to that used in a store. However, this terminal would be slightly larger than an authentic one so that it could fit over top of the real one. The fake terminal would allow an unsuspecting customer to swipe their card, enter their PIN, and complete the transaction. However, the fake terminal would also record the PIN and the information on the card's magnetic stripe. The fraudster would then retrieve the terminal after a few days and begin using the information to create duplicate cards. These fake terminals could be an overlay of a PIN pad at a theatre or convenience store, or could be as large and sophisticated as a complete front piece on a drive-through teller at a bank.

A gang of fraudsters used this last method as they travelled across Canada setting up false fronts on drive-through tellers. The culprits would install the false front and a camera in order to record the victim's PIN. These fraudsters would then do a quality check of the camera and the installation, which would also serve as a starting point to retrieve the information collected. They would then wait in a vehicle and monitor the false terminal until it was time to disconnect it and retrieve the data.

Another method involves using a card reader that can be concealed in a person's hand, or clipped on their belt, that will hold hundreds of numbers. When the card owner is distracted, or not looking, the fraudster swipes the card a second time and obtains the information. In either case, the card is swiped and the fake terminal records the information. The person's PIN is then obtained by use of a concealed "pin-hole" camera or by the fraudster "shoulder surfing," surreptitiously watching you enter your PIN.

As fraudsters become more advanced, other methods are emerging such as in-line interrupters between the terminal and the computer, or PIN pads that record the card info and the numbers pressed by the card owner.

What does a fraudster actually get when he skims a credit or debit card? The magnetic stripe on the back of a card contains a great deal of data encoded on two lines of information. This includes your bank information, branch and account number, your name, and other bits of data that allow the bank reader to identify your card.

A similar amount of information is also contained on hotel key locks that are now prevalent. Your name, address, and other information are encoded on these stripes. As a general rule, hotels do not erase the information that was encoded on the card when it is returned upon check-out. The cards are simply put into a box to be re-used and over-written when the next guest registers.

Fortunately, there are ways to protect yourself or limit your risk. Most fake pin-pad overlays are discovered by a customer using the terminal. Because they are usually secured with two-sided tape, the terminal often becomes dislodged. Don't be afraid to give the terminal a slight shake to make sure it is secure. Place passwords on your credit cards, bank, and phone accounts that only you would know. Do not make them family names or birthdays that the fraudster can easily obtain. Do not keep the passwords in your wallet or purse. Most financial institutions will not absorb the loss if the information was readily found or deciphered by the fraudster.

As mentioned, hotels have now begun using a swipe card in place of a traditional room key. However, these cards contain just as much information as your credit card. Many hotels no longer ask for the cards to be returned when you check out of the hotel. The cost of replacing a used card with a new blank one is minimal. If the hotel asks for the key card returned, insist that it be overwritten while you are standing there, to ensure that your information has been erased. When you get home, either cut up the card or use a magnet to erase the information from the magnetic stripe.

Secure personal information in your home by using a filing cabinet or safe. If you no longer need the information or forms, shred them before taking them to the recyclers. Cross-cut or multiple cut shredders are best, but the majority of fraudsters will not take the trouble to piece together ribbon-shredded paper, as there are easier, "softer," targets available.

Do not give out personal information on the phone or through the mail, unless you are sure of who is receiving the information. Most importantly, do not give out your Social Insurance Number as identification, or carry your card with you. Only financial institutions and government agencies have a legitimate need to use your Social Insurance Number. So keep it safe.

Guard your mail and trash and pay attention to billing cycles. If regular bills are late, contact the company and find out why. Perhaps you built up a credit on your bill, or perhaps it was intercepted.

Once a criminal has obtained information about you, he can now use that information to carry out other fraudulent and criminal activities in your name. Some of these activities include:

1. Obtaining a credit card in your name: False credit cards account for millions of lost revenue for banks and other financial institutions. Investigators may quickly determine that you are not the person responsible, but often only after you have received notification from a collection agency and several long, unpleasant conversations. Although you may not be required to pay the outstanding credit card charges, we all pay with increased service fees.

2. Obtaining phone service in your name: Similar to obtaining a credit card, obtaining cell phones or utility services also involve investigations that will not only leave you exhausted, but may also affect your own personal credit.

3. Opening bank accounts and writing cheques: Fraudsters can open bank accounts, transfer funds from your original account into a second account, withdraw the cash, or write bad cheques that not only affect your credit but also your good name. Often, small businesses will post a notice stating, "So and so, come in and pay your NSF cheque," telling the whole community that you are not reliable. Your reputation has been severely damaged at this point.

4. Filing for bankruptcy in your name: This would allow the fraudster to liquidate your assets and leave you holding the bag when the creditors start to come around to collect their property.

5. Obtaining loans for cars and goods: Also similar to obtaining a credit card or phone services, you are the one left to prove your non-involvement.

6. Giving your name to the police when arrested: A man who gave his brother's name when stopped by the police resulted in over forty outstanding warrants for the brother's arrest for traffic violations.

Another innocent man was arrested during a routine traffic stop while visiting the city with his wife and three-year-old child. There were outstanding warrants for his arrest for failing to attend court and for assault. Because it was a weekend, the man had to spend two nights in jail until he could attend court on Monday morning to prove that he was not the person named in the warrant. His wife and child had to stay at a hotel for the weekend before they could all go home together. Although these mistakes often get sorted out, the time, inconvenience, and the hardship this causes stays with that person for years.

12

FRAUDS FOR REVENGE

As mentioned in the first chapter, fraud is defined as deprivation through deception. This is what differentiates it from other crimes such as theft. We have looked at several elaborate schemes, including telemarketing fraud, recovery pitches, and identity thefts. But not all frauds are, or have to be, as sophisticated as those described. Sometimes the fraudster doesn't even think that he is committing a fraud.

The following case studies are examples of simple, relatively unsophisticated frauds committed against friends and family. In some cases, the fraudster was more interested in retaliating against the victim for a perceived wrong than obtaining a substantial monetary gain. Whether the wrong committed was real or imaginary, the "aggrieved party" still took matters into their own hands in seeking satisfaction. It usually resulted in being charged with a criminal offence. When people are caught up in revenge, they do not consider the consequences.

HEAVEN HAS NO RAGE LIKE
LOVE TO HATRED TURNED...,

Mel owned several businesses in the city, and he had often made purchases for his home through the business. Mel had put a number of shares for the businesses in his wife's name for tax purposes, although she was not involved in the operation of the businesses. When he and his wife, Natasha, separated in June, they completed a separation agreement, as there was no pre-nuptial agreement in place.

As a condition of the separation agreement, under the heading of "Business Interests," one of Mel's businesses was transferred to Natasha to provide her with an income. All shares and interests in the other businesses held by Natasha were transferred to Mel, making him the sole owner of these businesses and responsible for all details. One of the transferred businesses included Perfection Manufacturing Inc.

Natasha felt that Mel had used her. She had helped him in developing his businesses and that she was entitled to more than what was stipulated in the Separation Agreement. To show Mel that she was not someone who could be dismissed lightly, Natasha decided that she would get what she felt she deserved one way or another.

Natasha proceeded to purchase new furniture and building materials, both for her home and her business. She and Mel had used these companies in the past, so no questions were asked regarding her purchasing authority. It was only after requests for payment arrived that Mel discovered what Natasha had done.

Mel provided the police with copies of invoices placed by Natasha totaling $25,000 for furniture, supplies, and other items. In addition, on several occasions Natasha would show up at the business and take the mail, which included bills and invoices addressed to Perfection Manufacturing Inc. and Canadian Perfection Corp., both businesses still owned by Mel. According to some employees, Natasha would tear up the invoices and throw them in the garbage. Employees of Mel's actually witnessed these and later recovered the torn invoices and turned them over to Mel.

Mel stated to the police that this activity has caused his business loss of reputation and services because he was unable to pay these bills. The police consulted with the Crown Prosecutor's office and it was decided that this was a civil matter between a husband and wife and not in the interest of the public to pursue this case in a criminal court. No charges were filed against Natasha.

... NOR HELL A FURY LIKE A WOMAN SCORNED

Vanessa had been married to Tommy for nine years, and the couple had a seven-year-old boy. Tommy owned a contracting business that required him to work long hours while Vanessa stayed at home and raised their son. With the growing economy, Tommy's business began doing very well. As his business became more successful, Tommy had opportunities to expand into other areas. After nine years, Tommy decided that he would leave Vanessa because he had met someone else. In the separation agreement, Tommy agreed to provide child support of $2,000 per month for their son. However, Tommy was not always on time with the agreed support.

One afternoon, Tommy met with Vanessa and stated that he was no longer willing to pay the amount they had agreed upon for child support. Instead, Tommy gave Vanessa a cheque for $1,500 for that month. Vanessa was upset and hurt. Not only was this not fair, but Tommy thought he could get away with giving her a lesser amount. Vanessa looked at the cheque and saw that the dollar amount was not filled in. In his anger, he had signed the cheque but forgot to include an amount. Vanessa made the cheque out for $5,000.

When the cheque cleared Tommy's account, Tommy took the cheque to the police and wanted Vanessa charged with fraud. The police had little choice but to charge Vanessa. She admitted to filling in the $5,000 on the cheque because of the way Tommy had been treating her. Whether this was fair or not was not a factor the police could take into consideration. Vanessa received a $200 fine and two years probation, while Tommy is still late with his child support payments.

• • •

It is always easier to think of fraudsters as someone we don't know. Our friends and family are too close to us and would never jeopardize our relationship by stealing or lying. But what if that relationship goes sour and you bitterly part company?

In a general sense, spouses cannot steal from one another. Once you are married, or have been living together for some time, the property becomes communal and shared equally between the two. This also includes finances. However, if the couple should separate and, after the separation, one commits fraudulent activities, there may be a case for a criminal investigation.

Unfortunately, these types of fraud are very difficult for investigators and the courts to deal with, generally because of the ambiguity of the relationships. Both parties often make promises without writing them down, and the high emotions that are in play often end up as confusing and misunderstood statements.

Frequently, the party that contacts the police is not concerned with the money that has been lost. They are more interested in seeing what they perceive to be justice being done, and to have their ex-spouse punished and "taught a lesson." More likely than not, these situations are better dealt with through the assistance of a mediator, counselor, or a lawyer, and not through the criminal courts. A criminal investigation is not the best way to resolve the problem.

13

REAL ESTATE FRAUD, FALSE CHARITIES, AND OUTRIGHT LIES

MY HOME IS MY CASTLE

Nathan Francis had worked for Calgary Transit as a driver for over twenty years. In that time he had seen how the city was expanding and how the real estate market was steadily growing. While driving his route, Nathan would always note the houses that were for sale and how quickly they sold. One particular day Nathan noticed a home in the southwest area of the city that caught his fancy. He wrote down the number of the realtor and called her at the end of his shift that afternoon.

Bridgett Carey, the realtor for the southwest house, had been in the real estate business for fifteen years. She would buy and sell real estate as fast as she could list the property. When Nathan called, Bridgett knew she had another opportunity to make some money.

Nathan told Bridgett that he was interested in the house in the southwest and would like to know some more about it. Bridgett offered to meet with Nathan and his wife so they could look at the house and discuss things further. When Bridgett met with Nathan and his wife,

Nathan explained that they were only looking right now, but thought that the house might lead to an investment for them. Bridgett told them that real estate is always a good investment, but if they were not interested in living in the house, she might have another opportunity for them.

The house in the southwest was listed for $220,000. If Nathan was interested, Bridgett would pay him $1,000 to purchase the house, in name only, and then Bridgett would re-list the house for $235,000. It would be a quick turnaround sale for Bridgett, and Nathan would make an easy $1,000. As far as any down payments to the bank were concerned, Bridgett told Nathan that she had some partners who would put up the down payment while the house was being re-sold.

Nathan and his wife talked it over and thought this might be a good opportunity. Both had heard how people bought and sold, or flipped, houses and made a quick profit. Besides, Bridgett was a licensed realtor so what could go wrong? Nathan agreed and signed the forms that Bridgett gave him. He left most of the spaces blank because Bridgett told him that she would fill in the amounts at her office. Bridgett then gave Nathan a cheque for $1,000 and the deal was done.

When he agreed to Bridgett's scheme, Nathan became what is known as a straw-buyer. A straw-buyer is someone who is paid for the use of his or her name and credit information in order to make a fraudulent mortgage application. Most straw-buyers are paid several thousands of dollars for the use of their name and identity. A fraudster uses a straw-buyer in several ways:

- stating that the straw-buyer will reside in the property when there is no intention of doing so;
- claiming that the down payment has come from the straw-buyer's own funds; or
- signing documents that inflate the value of a property.

It should be noted that although there is usually another fraudster who is the architect behind this scheme, the straw-buyer is also guilty of committing fraud and may face criminal charges. Claiming that you did not know that your information was going to be used to commit mortgage fraud is not an excuse.

After a straw-buyer takes the title to the property, the fraudster behind the scheme usually assumes the mortgage and the title to the property. The fraudster will then sell the house or rent the property to someone for other criminal activity, such as a marijuana growing operation. If the mortgage payments are not paid, the lender may foreclose on the property to recover their losses. The straw-buyer may be sued for the amount owing on the mortgage and any legal fees and costs incurred by the lender.

Real estate fraud is rapidly becoming one of the most profitable forms of fraud in North America. First Canadian Title, a company that provides title insurance to consumers, estimates that real estate title fraud costs Canadians $300 million to $1.5 billion annually,[1] while law enforcement officials and lenders estimate that 10 to 15 percent of all mortgage applications contain false information.[2] There are two types of real estate fraud: mortgage fraud and title fraud.

Mortgage fraud, like the story involving Nathan and Bridgett, generally targets financial institutions that lend the money to purchase property. Mortgage fraud artificially increases the property value of a property by selling and reselling the property until the main fraudster behind the scheme decides to end the circle, make a final sale, and move on to another property. The end buyer becomes an innocent third-party victim when they try to sell the property to discover that the price was inflated and whose market value is less than the mortgage that they have. The fraudsters, if they are caught, often receive a minimal punishment, if any at all. Nathan was not charged for his part in the scheme because the financial institution determined that it was not worth their time and resources to pursue criminal charges against him. Bridgett had her realtor licence suspended for six months but also was not charged criminally.

In another case, Christopher and Janice had been married for two years and bought their first home with the help of both of their parents. They had been living in their house for three years, when one afternoon a real estate agent pulled up in front of their house and started to put a

"For Sale" sign on their lawn. It was only at this time Chris and Janice discovered that they had been made a victim of title fraud and that there was a lien placed on their property.

Title fraud is the most frightening form of real estate fraud for the individual homeowner because it targets them directly, and in many cases, it is easy. In a title fraud, the fraudster will use stolen identities or forged documents to transfer ownership of a property to themselves without the property owner knowing of the transfer. The fraudster obtains a mortgage on this title and, once the money is given to him, he disappears, leaving the property at risk of being foreclosed. In other cases, the fraudster will claim that they are owed money and will file documents with the court and have a lien placed on the property. The courts would enforce the lien because the victim would be unaware of it and not show in court to dispute the claim.

Once a title fraud has been committed, the burden of proving the deception is placed on the original homeowner. This means that it is usually up to the homeowners to prove that they are victims of title theft. This can often cost the homeowners thousands of dollars and several years to restore their title. As for the fraudster, he may or may not be charged. In the case of Chris and Janice, the fraudster received sixty days in jail to be served on weekends. He was also ordered by the court to repay Chris and Janice but has not done so.

When buying property, whether for an investment or to purchase a new home, there are several things that you can do to help protect yourself:

- Do your homework: Do your research on the Internet to determine the market value of the properties in the area. Compare the size, features, and locations to determine whether the price is reasonable.
- Use a licensed realtor and contact the real estate board to verify that they are licensed. Too often, we take a person's credentials at face value.
- Obtain a copy of the land title or ask the land title office to do a registry search. Usually a fee is involved for this service, but it could save you thousands of dollars and years of heartache.

- As a homeowner, check your own title on a regular basis. Ensure that there are no liens or title transfers placed on your property. Insurance companies are also offering title insurance for homeowners to help protect them and cover the costs of court proceedings to recover and keep your home.

GIVE 'TILL IT HURTS

Lindsay Barkhaus was not very successful in life. He could not hold down a job, his marriage was over, and he was alienated from the rest of his family. He was living day-to-day, just trying to get by. One day, Barkhaus came upon an idea to obtain money from the local bars.

Barkhaus printed some forms using a library computer, printer, and photocopier. He then went to the bars around his neighbourhood, asking for the manager. Barkhaus explained that he was the manager for the local men's baseball team, and that he was seeking sponsorship to help offset the cost of uniforms and rent for the sports fields. In return, he would guarantee that his team, and their opponents, would frequent the bar after the games. After all, the amount of beer they would drink would easily make up for any donation made by the bar, plus the bar could use the donation as a write-off for promotion.

Barkhaus had it all worked out in his proposal — how much uniforms would cost (with and without advertising), the cost of renting the field, the cost of umpires, etc. For a small investment of $1,500, the bar could sponsor the team in the coming season. Barkhaus failed to mention that there was no men's baseball team that he was managing.

Meanwhile, during the day Barkhaus was working another scheme. Several years previously, a fundraising company had hired Barkhaus to canvass for the Canadian Teenage Pregnancy Support Society (CTPSS) based in Toronto. Barkhaus was provided with a campaign kit containing promotional material and donation receipt books. But like all of Barkhaus' other jobs, this one did not last long. However, when Barkhaus left, he failed to return the campaign kit.

Barkhaus continued to travel door to door asking for donations to help educate, house, and clothe young girls who were single parents. He would show the promotional material to the donor and would issue a charitable tax receipt. For a donation of $10, the donor would obtain a tax receipt and would be helping these young girls. When Barkhaus ran out of original receipts from the campaign kit, he reproduced more receipts using a photocopier. Unfortunately, the money Barkhaus collected would not go back to the CTPSS.

Unscrupulous criminals will often take advantage of natural disasters or tragic events to defraud people. They will pose as canvassers for a charitable organization and ask for a donation. Often, the donation is for a small amount of money, $5 to $10. This is an amount that will not be missed or an amount too small for the victim to bother the police about.

Some of these fraudsters will invent names that sound similar to a legitimate organization in order to deceive those of us generous enough to donate to a cause. Others, like Lindsay, will even have props, such as photocopies of tax receipts, to assist in carrying out their scheme.

If you receive a request to donate to a charity, either by telephone or from a door-to-door canvasser, here are a few points to consider:

1. Decide which charities you wish to support and the amount you can afford to donate, then send your cheques directly to their head office. When approached by a canvasser you can tell them that you have already supported your choice of charities.

2. Ask for identification. Legitimate canvassers have proper identification that includes their name, the organization, and a contact number for the charity. Often they will also have a city licence or permit to allow the charity to canvass in that area on that specific day.

3. Determine if the canvasser has any knowledge of how your donation will be used. Do they know how much of your donation will go toward administrative costs and what percentage will go towards the actual charity? Legitimate charities and canvassers will have some idea of these distributions and will have no

problem giving you this information.

4. If you receive a solicitation by telephone, ask for the information to be sent to you.

5. Never give your personal or financial information over the phone or at the door. Obtain the information and mail the cheque later.

6. If you have any questions don't be afraid to call the charity. Find out if they are aware of canvassers in your area. At this time you can also find out more details and how your donation will be distributed. You may find that there is a way to support this charity that better suits you.

7. Always ask for a tax receipt. Not only will this help you when consolidating your records, but it can also be used by investigators should you fall victim to a false charity scheme.

I AM WHAT I AM

It was a warm spring morning when Madelyn Burton entered the Petite Louvre Art Gallery in downtown Victoria, British Columbia. The Petite Louvre was a store specializing in fine art for home and office. Burton had spotted some art in the window that she would love to have for her office. When she entered the showroom, Christine, the assistant manager, greeted her and offered to help her select pieces that would suit Burton's style and personality.

Burton told Christine that she was a successful advertising and promotions advisor and that she had moved to the city from Toronto six weeks earlier. Most of Burton's office furniture stayed behind in Toronto at her other office. Burton now wanted something new and vibrant that would show her clients that she was here to do business. Burton selected several items, including a crystal floor vase, some lamps, and other accent pieces. She arranged to have them delivered to her condo overlooking the park, and gave Christine her business card and a cheque to complete the deal.

That afternoon, Burton went to the Electronix First shop and purchased a new Macintosh computer, a Macintosh laptop to use when she was on the road, and a PDA to help her keep track of her appointments and clients. Burton had the store carry out these items to her Mercedes and put into the trunk. She would have the concierge at the condo help her bring the new computer into her condo.

Burton also went to two different furniture stores and purchased a new bedroom suite and a classically designed modern roll-top desk for her office. These were also to be delivered to Burton's apartment. Burton again provided her business cards and a cheque to cover the down payment, with the balance due once the furniture arrived safely. Burton told the salesperson that she had had an experience in Toronto, where her living-room suite arrived with chips and it took her months to get it replaced.

Burton also visited the Art1 Gallery to purchase some pieces for her new home and office. Art1 Gallery was another store that specialized in North American artists and had locations in New York, Vancouver, Victoria, Calgary, Toronto, and Halifax. Burton met with Robin, the assistant manager, and selected fourteen pieces that she adored. Burton reminded Robin that Art1 had a contract with Burton's company in Toronto and arranged to have her new purchases delivered to her condo. In all, Burton's three-day shopping excursion totaled over $175,500 in art work, furniture, and accessories.

Two weeks after Burton's visit to Petite Louvre Gallery, Christine was notified by her bank that Burton's cheque could not be honoured. The account, located in Thunder Bay, Ontario, had closed two years earlier and had no activity on it in that period. Christine grew concerned and called Burton.

Burton was appalled that the cheque had bounced. She had gathered all of her banking records when she moved west and must have inadvertently picked up the wrong chequebook when she went out that day. Burton promised she would be in the next morning to correct the problem.

The next morning came and went without Burton showing at the gallery. Christine made several unsuccessful attempts to contact her. All she could get was Burton's answering machine. After a month of leaving messages and getting no response from Burton, Christine contacted the police.

While Burton was furnishing her condo and office, another fraudster across the city, Stephen Inman, was in the process of completing a $75,000 deal on five electric generators with Vaughan Agencies. Inman was in his late fifties and was used to industrial equipment. He had been a heavy equipment driver for ten years. He had worked on and driven just about everything that could be found in a heavy equipment lot.

One day, Inman was driving by the yards of Vaughan Agencies when he spotted five industrial generators in the yard. It looked like the generators had been in the yard for a few months, and Inman saw an opportunity. Inman went into the offices of Vaughan Agencies and met with Kurt, the inventory manager for Vaughan. Inman presented himself as a heavy equipment broker and stated that he had a customer for five generator sets. Because the generators had been sitting in the yard for so long, it was easy to convince Kurt to sell him the generators.

Inman explained that this sale was actually to be part of a larger deal involving twenty-one pieces of equipment, valued at over $175,000. Inman then produced a large roll of bills, which he began to give to Kurt, stating that it was a $20,000 cash down payment for the generators. Kurt refused to take the cash, as he wanted a cheque to allow a paper trail.

Inman then offered his Rolex watch and his ring, again supposedly valued at $20,000, as collateral, but Kurt again refused. Inman then wrote Kurt a cheque on his business account, Re-New Equipment, for the entire $75,000. Inman told Kurt that he would return with a certified cheque, as their original bargain called for. Inman's cheque was subsequently returned as NSF.

Prior to meeting with Kurt, Inman had made a similar deal with Hamilton Equipment in Cape Breton. Inman had contacted Hamilton Equipment and arranged for a shipment of equipment valued at $60,000 to be sent to Inman for another client. A certified cheque was sent to Hamilton Equipment and the equipment was delivered. When this cheque was also returned as NSF, Hamilton Equipment went looking for Inman. As it eventually turned out, Inman had sold the equipment to several construction sites in northern Alberta and the Northwest Territories.

When Burton and Inman met with their victims, each of them told a story of who they were and what they represented. The victims took their story at face value because they were able to talk in the language of the business, and they both provided the props to help complete the deception. In Burton's case, it was the business cards. In Inman's, it was the company cheques and the roll of money. Kurt never did examine the money to see if it was all twenties or whether the watch really was a Rolex.

Fraudsters like Burton and Inman are in for the quick buy and sell. They will generally have some buyers ready to purchase what they have to offer. Often, these buyers believe that they are legitimate brokers. When Burton's condo was searched, the computers, furniture, and art were already gone. The fourteen pictures were in the process of being removed from their frames in preparation for shipment.

Two of Vaughan Agencies' generators were in the Alberta oil sands, but without serial numbers, they were untraceable. It is important to realize that things, and appearances, are not always what they appear to be.

I CAN MAKE YOU INTO ANYONE YOU WANT TO BE

Hong Ma was a first generation Asian, whose family immigrated to Canada in the 1960s. He obtained his B.A. in Commerce at the University of New Brunswick and had a successful online business where he employed eight people. Ma enjoyed the life of a successful, good-looking male in Fredericton, New Brunswick. He went to the clubs and casinos, making friends and enjoying life.

Ma came up with an idea to forge insurance cheques and get them cashed at the banks before they knew what hit them. If he used insurance companies as the payee, the banks would most likely pass them, because insurance companies often pay out larger sums of money.

To complete his plan, Ma needed some associates that were in need of ready cash, would not ask too many questions, and whom he could manipulate. The answer was staring him in the face at the nightclubs. Ma would recruit young college and university students for his scheme.

Ma approached Stacey and her friend Kimberly, asking if they would be interested in earning $300 each. Ma explained that he was targeting the banks because they were just an extension of the government and that they could afford to lose the money. Besides, with all of the useless bank charges and hidden bills, everyone deserved to get something back. Stacey and Kim agreed with Ma's sentiments and agreed to go along and help him. Back at Ma's apartment, Stacey and Kim took advantage of Ma's offer of cocaine while Ma began setting up the equipment. There was a digital camera, two computers, a photo printer, and an embossing machine. There was also a machine that printed onto white plastic cards, the size of a credit card.

Ma took the two girls' driver licences and scanned them into his system. He then took each of the girls' pictures and downloaded them into the program as well. Ma then created new identities for the girls, changed the addresses and birthdates, and printed out forty-five new driver's licences for each of the girls. He then created similar social insurance number cards for each of the same ninety identities. Ma then took the girls to their homes and told them he would be in touch.

Once the girls had left, Ma returned to his apartment, where he began the task of printing cheques. He opened a box of blank cheques he had bought online in the United States. Such cheques and the plastic cards are lawfully sold to small businesses. He then scanned the logos of various insurance companies into his computer and created cheques in amounts from $16,578.13 to $34,784.68, payable to the identities that he created for Stacey and Kim.

Ma figured that the cheques would appear more believable if they were for odd amounts rather than a rounded number. He then batched the driver's licences, corresponding SIN cards and the forged insurance cheques into envelopes. He then called Stacey and told her he would pick her up in an hour.

Stacey and Ma first went to the Royal Bank in downtown Fredericton, where Stacey entered the bank. She explained to the customer service representative that she would be receiving an insurance settlement for a car accident she had had last year. She wanted to open an account so that when the cheque arrived, she could deposit it. The customer service representative was sympathetic to Stacey because she had been involved in a car accident four years earlier and was still suffering from the injuries.

An account was opened in Stacey's false name and photocopies of her identification were taken. Stacey then received a temporary bank card so that she could access her account whenever she wanted. On Friday, Stacey deposited her first cheque for $19,267.67. She and Ma continued this charade twenty-three more times, all under different names and all for various amounts. Ma followed the same pattern with Kim.

The following week, Ma met with Kim and Stacey and began to withdraw money from the accounts. The girls would enter the bank and present their bank card and identification and withdraw the money, usually leaving a few hundred dollars in the account. Sometimes they would withdraw the cash through the automatic bank machine.

Ma would then count out $300 for each transaction and keep the rest. He would also provide a hit or two of cocaine as a bonus for the girls' good work. This sequence continued over a two-week period until one customer service representative became suspicious and called the Fredericton police, who arrested Ma and another one of his accomplices.

When the police executed a search warrant on Ma's apartment, they discovered all of the equipment, blank cards, cheques, and computer programs that Ma had used. The police also found $13,000 cash and twelve more sets of identification for other people, as well as over thirty individually packaged hits of cocaine. Over the next several months, the banks in Fredericton, St. John, and Moncton confirmed that the identities discovered by the Fredericton police had opened up accounts and made deposits. Fortunately, the bank's losses were kept minimal because of the quick action of the Fredericton Police and the alert customer service representative.

Ma was held overnight in jail pending his court appearance the next morning. He was released on $500 bail and a promise to appear in court, for which he failed to appear. The police used the newspapers and television news to ask for the public's help in identifying Ma's twelve accomplices. Nine of the twelve were positively identified, including Stacey and Kim. Of these nine, four were charged and found guilty, each receiving a $750 fine, while arrest warrants were issued for four more, including Kim. Stacey pled guilty, provided a statement to the police, and received an unconditional discharge.

IT SEEMED LIKE THE PERFECT VACATION

Noelle was a stay-at-home mother looking for a part-time job to help with the expenses of her two small children. Noelle had seen an ad in the paper advertising for telephone persons interested in working at home. Successful applicants would be paid $10 per hour and could obtain bonuses for completed sales. The ad did not name the company and gave only a phone number to contact. Noelle thought that this would do the trick for her, and called the number.

Noelle was forwarded to a person who stated that his name was Nick, the president of MDC Properties. Nick explained that MDC Properties was a vacation rental and time share company with real estate in Canada and the United States. Nick asked a few simple questions of Noelle and explained that her job would be to receive phone calls forwarded to her and to set up potential bookings for properties. When it came time to close the deal, Noelle would pass the information on to Nick, who would make the final arrangements. Noelle was hired in less than ten minutes over the phone.

Gordon and Debbie had been planning their perfect vacation in Maine for years. They would rent a Cape Cod home on the shore and watch the waves crash into the bluffs in front of the house as they sat on the white Adirondack chairs on the porch. They would indulge themselves and pretend to be living the life of the Great Gatsby. But, as is often the case with such dreams, the expense for this type of vacation was out of their reach for the time being.

One afternoon, Debbie was surfing the web, dreaming of their vacation, when she came across a website for rental vacation properties. The website was managed by MDC Properties. They had a listing of over 120 properties for rent throughout the United States. One link was to Maine Properties and when Debbie went to the site, there was the cottage that she and Gordon had dreamed of.

Debbie had heard of the types of schemes that were offered on the Internet, and she did not want to be disappointed. She called the number on the website and spoke to a customer service representative, Noelle. Noelle explained that MDC was a vacation real estate consortium that rented properties from clients across the United States. These properties would then be offered as vacation packages when the owners would not be using the property. The consortium acted very much like a time-share program, but without the restrictions that a time-share imposes.

Debbie was told that the cost for two weeks at the Maine property was $4,500, plus taxes, but she would have to be contacted by the president to complete the final arrangements and bookings. Two days later, Debbie received a telephone call from Nick, who wanted to close the deal with Debbie. Yes, the property was available on the dates that she wanted. There was a non-refundable deposit of 33 percent required with the balance due four weeks before the possession date.

Debbie was instructed to print the application form from the website, complete the form, and mail it to the MDC offices with her cheque. Once MDC received full payment, Debbie would receive a package in the mail containing all instructions, maps, and keys for the property two weeks before her holiday.

Debbie followed Nick's instructions. She and Gordon booked their vacations, flights to Maine, and looked forward to the holiday. Four weeks before the vacation Debbie sent the second payment and anxiously looked forward to her vacation package. Two weeks came and went and there was no package from MDC Properties. Another week passed, and still no package arrived. Debbie called the telephone number that she had used before, and only received a voicemail message. The next day, the voicemail box was full.

Debbie and others had fallen victim to a vacation scheme that appeared legitimate, but was all a hoax. The properties listed were actual properties, but they were listed with companies other than MDC. The pictures and descriptions had been downloaded from other sites on the Internet and linked into the MDC Properties website. Noelle was "hired" but was never paid and was not aware that this was a scheme. When contacted, she readily provided the police with a record of all her calls and contacts to assist in their investigation.

Nick had used a virtual office to re-route his calls to Noelle. He also used this office as his mailing address and as a location for his faxes. Unfortunately, no one at the virtual office had ever met Nick and all mail was picked up by a courier.

As it turned out, hundreds of victims lost their money and down payments to MDC Properties and Nick. What was worse, these victims also lost their vacation, flights, and other bookings that were made in conjunction with their vacation because they no longer had a place to stay for their two weeks.

Debbie and Gordon were luckier than most. Although they lost their initial deposit, the police intercepted one hundred envelopes containing cheques made out to MDC Properties and retuned them to the originators of the cheques. The use of couriers and a virtual office meant the police were unable to identify anyone responsible for this scam. Although Federal agents in the United States have linked this scheme to a larger venture operating in Los Angles and Reno, to date no arrests have been made and the culprits are still unknown.

The best thing about the Internet is that it allows you to search the entire world for just about anything you can imagine. From vacation properties, to cars, to tickets for sports and other special events, they are all available on the web. But, as we have seen, there are also unscrupulous people who will take advantage of your trust to take your money.

When purchasing items from the Internet, do your research. When you find an item that catches your interest, do specific searches on the item that is being offered. You can also do a search on the company and the names of the people listed with the company. It is possible to use the Internet to your advantage to determine truth from deception.

After you have completed your search and gathered as much information as you can, ask the people offering the service you are interested in questions about the product and the company. Find out where they are located or if they have a list of satisfied customers that you can contact. If the company is legitimate, they will be able to provide answers to all of your questions. Be wary of vague answers or attempts to conceal information. This may be an indication that the company or the person is not genuine.

14

WHO YOU GONNA CALL?

With the huge financial potential, there is an increasing trend for organized crime to become involved in telemarketing frauds. Not only does this provide these criminals with a lucrative cash flow, but it also allows organized crime to fund other criminal activity such as narcotics, prostitution, and gunrunning.

The traditional role of the police is to carry out their duties, such as detecting and solving crime, patrolling the streets in their vehicles or on foot, enforce traffic regulations, and so on. These duties are generally confined to legislated jurisdictional areas, such as municipal, regional, provincial, or federal boundaries. Although there are protocols and agreements in place to allow police officers to operate outside their jurisdiction, this often becomes time consuming and an administrative burden. However, with the ever-shrinking world through the Internet, cellular phones, and rapid transit, the role of the police had to dramatically change to keep up with the criminal element.

Interpol's definition of organized crime is: "Any enterprise or group of persons engaged in a continuing illegal activity, which has, as its primary purpose, the generation of profits regardless of national boundaries."[1] This emphasizes the transitional cross-border concept that police services in Canada are now only learning to face. Up to now, municipal police agencies have confined their efforts and resources to their jurisdictional boundaries as defined within their respective Police Acts.

The Alberta Police Act, for example, authorizes a municipal officer authority within the municipality and within the Province of Alberta. However, it does provide for circumstances should a police member be required to leave the province. Generally, this provision grants the status of special constable during the period of time that the officer is outside the province.

The RCMP, due to their status as a federal policing agency, does not have these inter-provincial restrictions. The problems of traditional policing response for municipal police and the RCMP only become compounded when faced with international borders.

Illegal telemarketing that crosses borders and targets Canadian and American citizens has required the Canadian and United States governments and agencies within these countries to develop a multi-faceted response. Canada and the United States have implemented significant changes in their laws on money laundering and proceeds of crime, as well as bolstering existing laws. Such changes allow agencies to seize proceeds of crime based upon reasonable grounds that they were obtained through the commission of a criminal act.

Law enforcement agencies have begun to adapt innovative strategies to combat the increase in telemarketing fraud by establishing Mutual Legal Assistance Treaties (MLATs) that allow cross-jurisdictional cooperation. A MLAT provides a legal framework that allows law enforcement agencies in other countries to share information regarding investigations and to obtain statements and evidence that would be admissible in a court proceeding. Multi-agency task forces and strategic partnerships such as Project COLT in Quebec, Project EMPTOR in Vancouver, and the FBI's Operation Canadian Eagle work to target mass-marketing fraud, share intelligence, and coordinate investigation and enforcement.

In Canada, there are seven partnerships whose primary function is to address cross-border fraud. Partnership make-up consists of the municipal police agencies within the province, the Royal Canadian Mounted Police, the Ontario Provincial Police or the Sûreté du Québec, the Competition Bureau of Industry Canada, Provincial Fair Trade or Government Services Departments, the United States Postal Inspection Service, and the United States Fair Trade Commission.

As an example, the Alberta Partnership Against Cross-Border Fraud consists of investigators from the RCMP, Calgary and Edmonton Police Services, Service Alberta, the United States Fair Trade Commission, and the United States Postal Inspection Service. The Partnership meets formally quarterly to review current cases, share information, and determine whether an investigation falls within their mandate to investigate, based upon a predetermined formula.

Once the Partnership decides to investigate a case as a partnership file, then the appropriate resources are allotted to the case. These resources can take several forms, such as funds to pay informants or establish surveillance, interview victims in different provinces or states, or track and freeze assets in the culprit's possession.

Other organizations, such as PhoneBusters, a joint venture between the Ontario Provincial Police Anti-Racketeering Squad and the Royal Canadian Mounted Police, the United States Consumer Sentinel, and NW3C (National White Collar Crime Center), serve as a focal point for intelligence gathering, tracking of trends, information resource, and public awareness. Finally, public advisories about telemarketing frauds and media releases on special task forces and high-profile arrests combine to educate the public.

When reporting a fraudulent occurrence, most local municipal police services have a dedicated commercial crime and fraud or economic crimes unit. The members of these units are trained in forensic accounting and have an expertise in financial investigations, to which most regular members are not exposed. Sadly, these specialized investigators and units are too often underfunded and undermanned. The amount of time and money required to train a fraud investigator can be prohibitive to law enforcement agencies for the return that they would get on their investment. Investigators would leave after a period of three to five years to pursue other opportunities that would lead to recognition and promotion.

Commercial crime or fraud units are often described within the policing community as the "poor step-sister" of a major crimes division of a police service. The facts of the matter are that auditing bank statements and processing boxes of paper does not have the pizzazz of other high-profile or violent crimes. Televised news coverage of a police SWAT team breaking down a door to seize drugs or weapons captivates audiences. Gang shootings and homicides attract the attention of the public and the administrations responsible for determining budgets and allocating finances to combat crime. Stories dealing with frauds, unless the frauds are in the millions of dollars or involve a prominent figure, are too often treated as public service announcements and consumer advisories.

An average convenience store robbery, although frightening and traumatic to the victim of the robbery, would net the culprit $50 to $100, plus some merchandise such as cigarettes. Police units would be dispatched immediately to the scene, a canine unit would likely attend, and then the crime scene investigators would also attend to take photographs and fingerprints. Other police units would be assigned to patrol the area and check any vehicles or pedestrians in the area, while still others would canvass the area to locate and interview witnesses. All of these things, and perhaps more, are necessary to investigate the crime, apprehend the culprit, and bring the case to trial. As for the robbery victim, the money may not be theirs if they do not own the store, and with some counselling, the victim can often resume their life as before.

An average fraud, on the other hand, will steal $5,000 to $10,000 from a victim. This loss is seldom covered by a person's insurance and may take the victim years to recoup the loss. To report the fraud, the victim would have to travel to a police office where the initial report would be taken and then forwarded to the fraud investigators. At the fraud office, the case is reviewed to determine if it meets established criteria for the fraud unit to investigate. Some of these criteria would include the possibility of identifying a suspect, the reliability of the victim, and the actual amount of the fraud. Some police agencies will not investigate a fraud if the amount the victim has lost is less than $10,000. If the case does pass the criteria for investigation, it will be assigned to an investigator who will add it to his or her active case files. It is a sad state of affairs that the majority of fraud investigators have over one hundred active case files at any given time. This regularly means that a fraud file will not even be looked at for up to eighteen months after it has been reported. A large number of those files will never be investigated further and the file inactivated.

Although this reality paints a depressing picture for a victim of fraud, you should still report the occurrence to your police department. Because of the natural makeup of frauds and the characteristics of both the schemes and the criminals carrying out these frauds, often schemes will overlap and tie into other investigations. Sometimes it might take one seemingly unrelated file to put all of the pieces in a larger file together, which may lead to charges and a conviction.

Because of the restraints involved in investigating frauds and the unlikelihood that fraud victims will recover any of their money you have to be aware of these schemes and know how to avoid them. The following are precautions you can take to protect yourself or to limit your risk of becoming a victim, whether the fraudster uses the Internet, the telephone, or newspaper ads:

- Wait before you commit to sending any money. A twenty-four or forty-eight hour period to rethink things is not unreasonable. Remember, the fraudster will try to put pressure on you to send the money right away. Do not give in to this pressure; after all, it is your money.
- While not giving in to the pressure, take the time to do some research. Search the Internet and ask to speak to other people in the company. Call the Better Business Bureau and your police department. Fraud investigators generally are aware of current schemes and may have heard of a similar occurrence. Most investigators will provide you with as much information as they can, keeping in mind the various privacy legislations. However, from their point of view, it is much easier to prevent a fraud from happening than to investigate a file months after the incident.

- Look into the possibility of protection through insurance. Several companies now offer insurance to help protect your identity, property title, and loss due to criminal activity. A number of insurance companies also provide financial assistance to cover the costs of legal fees associated with recovery.

There are many opportunities for you to profit in a small business, find your perfect vacation, or that item you have been searching for. After all of the research is done and you have enjoyed the fruits of your labour, the feeling can be just like receiving a special present on Christmas. Just remember to watch out for the Grinches.

APPENDIX

INVESTIGATOR'S TOOLS FOR FIGHTING FRAUD

1. THE MASS-MARKETING FRAUD REPORT TO THE ATTORNEY GENERAL OF THE UNITED STATES AND THE SOLICITOR GENERAL OF CANADA (MAY 2003).

In the report's Bi-national Action Plan for Cross Border Fraud, twelve points were summarized in such areas as strategies, operational efforts, information sharing, coordination between public and private sectors, and training. In respect to operational efforts, concerns were raised in the 1997 report on United States–Canada Working Group on Telemarketing Fraud about the efficiency of the process for obtaining formal assistance under the Mutual Legal Assistance Treaty (MLAT). It was recommended in the 2003 report that in addition to sharing under MLAT in appropriate circumstances, "agencies should continue to expand other efforts to assist each other's investigations, especially where agencies with civil authority, such as the FTC, are unable to use the (criminal) MLAT mechanism to coordinate with agencies that have either civil or criminal authority (or both)."

2. CANADA'S TELEMARKETING FRAUD "HAVEN"

The transparent and indefensible borders of telecommunications create opportunities for the criminal community. Historically, governments were concerned with the physical restrictions of the smuggling of goods (such as the rum running between Canada and the United States during Prohibition), illegal immigration, and the escape of felons by crossing into other countries. However, the seamless transfer of funds through electronic means, and the contacting and victimization of innocent victims through telephone, mail, and Internet has created challenges that have taxed the imagination of the authorities in order to combat these criminals.

This was vividly demonstrated in a statement made by Steven Baker of the U.S. Federal Trade Commission: "A large amount of the fraud that comes into the United States over the telephone comes from Canada."

"As well, Canadian penalties for those convicted of telephone fraud are not as stiff as those in the United States," Baker said. "Offenders convicted under U.S. law can be sentenced to five years in prison for each defrauded victim, while anyone convicted in Canada usually receives a fine or short prison term. Telemarketing fraud is a problem of international proportions that is being made worse by the Internet," said Baker.[1]

3. PHONEBUSTERS

Established in January of 1993, PhoneBusters is a national anti-fraud call centre jointly operated by the Ontario Provincial Police and the Royal Canadian Mounted Police. PhoneBusters plays a key role in educating the public about specific fraudulent telemarketing pitches. The call centre also plays a vital role in the collection and dissemination of victim evidence, statistics, documentation, and tape recordings which are made available to outside law enforcement agencies.

The original mandate of PhoneBusters was to prosecute key individuals in Ontario and Quebec involved in telemarketing fraud under the Criminal Code of Canada. Their mandate now also includes facilitating prosecution by United States agencies through extradition, and by the Competition Bureau under the Competition Act.

PhoneBusters is the central agency in Canada that collects information on telemarketing, advance fee fraud letters (Nigerian letters), and identity theft complaints. The information is disseminated to the appropriate law enforcement agencies. The data collected at PhoneBusters is a valuable tool in evaluating the effects of various types of fraud on the public. It also helps to prevent future similar crimes from taking place.[2]

4. EQUIFAX

Equifax Canada Inc. has been enabling business transactions since 1919. They are recognized in the consumer and commercial credit reporting and information services industry. Today, Equifax delivers sophisticated decision, data, fraud, and e-commerce solutions to the business community, which in turn allows Canadians to conveniently participate in millions of financial transactions daily.

Equifax customers include banks, retailers, wholesalers, manufacturers, government agencies, insurance companies, public utilities, and diversified financial services organizations.

Equifax Canada Inc. is a subsidiary of Atlanta-based Equifax Inc., a worldwide leader in enabling and securing global commerce. Equifax employs 4,800 people in twelve countries and has $1.1 billion in revenue.[3]

5. UNITED STATES POSTAL INSPECTION SERVICE

The United States Postal Inspection Service is one of the United States' oldest federal law enforcement agencies. Founded by Benjamin Franklin, the United States Postal Inspection Service has a long, proud, and successful history of fighting criminals who attack the U.S. postal system and misuse it to defraud, endanger, or otherwise threaten the American public. As the primary law enforcement arm of the United

States Postal Service, the U.S. Postal Inspection Service is a highly specialized, professional organization performing investigative and security functions essential to a stable and sound postal system.

Congress empowered the Postal Service "to investigate postal offences and civil matters relating to the Postal Service." Through its security and enforcement functions, the Postal Inspection Service provides assurance to American businesses for the safe exchange of funds and securities through the U.S. Mail to postal customers of the "sanctity of the seal" in transmitting correspondence and messages and to postal employees of a safe work environment.

As fact-finding and investigative agents, Postal Inspectors are federal law enforcement officers who carry firearms, make arrests, and serve federal search warrants and subpoenas. Inspectors work closely with U.S. Attorneys, other law enforcement agencies, and local prosecutors to investigate postal cases and prepare them for court. There are approximately 1,970 Postal Inspectors stationed throughout the United States who enforce more than two hundred federal laws covering investigations of crimes that adversely affect or fraudulently use the U.S. Mail and postal system.[4]

6. FINTRAC

The Financial Transactions and Reports Analysis Centre of Canada, or FINTRAC, is Canada's financial intelligence unit; a specialized agency created to collect, analyze, and disclose financial information and intelligence on suspected money laundering and the financing of terrorist activities. Created in July 2000, it reports to Parliament through the Minister of Finance. The Centre is an integral part of Canada's engagement in the global fight against money laundering and the financing of terrorist activities.

The Centre was created to detect and deter money laundering by providing critical information to support the investigation or prosecution of money laundering offences. In December 2001, this mandate was expanded to include the detection and deterrence of terrorist activity financing.

More specifically, FINTRAC's mandate is to:

- receive and collect reports on suspicious and prescribed financial transactions and other information relevant to money laundering and terrorist activities financing;
- receive reports on the cross-border movement of large amounts of currency or monetary instruments;
- analyze and assess the information it receives;
- provide law enforcement financial intelligence that would be relevant to the investigation or prosecution of money laundering offences and terrorist activity financing offences as well as to provide CSIS with financial intelligence that would be relevant to threats to the security of Canada;
- ensure that personal information under its control is protected from unauthorized disclosure;
- ensure compliance by financial intermediaries and other reporting entities with their obligations under the Act and regulations; and
- enhance public awareness and understanding of matters related to money laundering and terrorist financing.

FINTRAC's Mission is to provide law enforcement and intelligence agencies with financial intelligence on money laundering, terrorist activity financing, and threats to the security of Canada, while ensuring the protection of the information it holds.[5]

7. PRODUCTION ORDERS

Production orders came into effect in October 2004 to address the limitations that exist with the Section 487 Search Warrants. Traditionally, search warrants were the only mechanism available for a fraud investigator to use when searching and seizing bank documents.

The limitation to a general warrant was that the items to be searched were believed to be at the location indicated on the search warrant on the date specified. This often would lead to investigators devising surreptitious means of ensuring that the documents would be available when they executed the warrant. It also required that the investigator have knowledge of specific information, such as the bank account number, prior to the creating of the warrant. Fortunately there has not been a serious challenge to these search warrants and they were used extensively.

A production order, on the other hand, is in essence a search warrant for documentary evidence. Section 487.012 of the Criminal Code allows for a production order to obtain general information such as date of birth and account numbers. Section 487.013 allows for a production order to obtain documentary evidence of a much broader scope. It also allows the use of the 487.012 production order as a source for obtaining information such as account numbers.

The principal advantages of a production order are two-fold. First, the production order recognizes that documents are rarely stored in a central or even local depository. A production order allows for a time period for the person named in the order to collect the information and make it available to the investigator. The second advantage allows substantial penalties for institutions that fail to comply or are negligent in providing the information requested. It should be noted, however, that production orders were not designed to be used on a suspect organization. Documentary evidence held by a suspect still requires a search warrant.

8. CRIMINAL CODE OF CANADA FRAUD DEFINITION

380. (1) Every one who, by deceit, falsehood or other fraudulent means, whether or not it is a false pretence within the meaning of this Act, defrauds the public or any person, whether ascertained or not, of any property, money or valuable security or any service,

    (a) is guilty of an indictable offence and liable to a term of imprisonment not exceeding ten years, where the subject-matter of the offence is a testamentary instrument or the value of the subject-matter of the offence exceeds five thousand dollars; or

(b) is guilty
    (i) of an indictable offence and is liable to imprisonment for a term not exceeding two years, or
    (ii) of an offence punishable on summary conviction, where the value of the subject-matter of the offence does not exceed five thousand dollars.

In simple terms, fraud can be considered as "deprivation through deception."

9. PROCEEDS OF CRIME (MONEY LAUNDERING) AND TERRORIST FINANCING ACT (CANADA)

The Proceeds of Crime and Terrorist Financing Act is an Act to facilitate combating the laundering of proceeds of crime, combating the financing of terrorist activities, to establish the Financial Transactions and Reports Analysis Centre of Canada, and to amend and repeal certain Acts in consequence.

10. UNIFORM RESOURCE LOCATOR

A Uniform Resource Locator (URL) specifies the location of and is the address of a file or resource accessible on the Internet. It is also called the "domain name" of the website or resource. An example of a URL would be *www.trustme.ca*.

11. VOICE OVER INTERNET PROTOCOL (VOIP)

Voice over Internet Protocol, or VoIP, allows a person to use the Internet to make long-distance telephone calls without the long-distance charges that are applied by the telephone companies. VoIP converts the voices into data for transmission over data networks. At the receiving end, the data is once again converted back into audio. There are several private VoIP providers in Canada and the United States.

12. VIRTUAL PHONE NUMBERS

Virtual phone numbers are secondary numbers that ring to your primary line. How does it work? Say your primary number has area code 613. By using a VoIP provider, you can select a virtual phone number in area code 403. When you call out, or someone calls you, the 403 number will ring to your 613 number to protect your information.

GLOSSARY

419 Letters: 419 letters are the term given to the letters and e-mails asking for money to perpetuate a scam. These are also referred to as advance fee letters. 419 is the section of the Nigerian Criminal Code for fraud offences. Most letters imply a sense of urgency and offer profits in the millions of dollars. *See also* **Nigerian Letters**.

900 Scams: The 900 scams are a variation on a prize pitch scheme. The potential victim is contacted, often through the mail, announcing that they have just won a large prize; either cash, a car, a boat, or a vacation.

The offer usually states that a brief phone call is required to collect your prize, and the cost of the call per minute is around $4.99. The victim is instructed to call a 1-900 number in order to find out how much money or what prize they have won. Most of these numbers are linked to a computerized voice response system, and the length of the call can last up to ten minutes without you realizing it. Once the call is completed and your information is confirmed, you may actually get a prize in the mail. Unfortunately, the prize sent is usually worth one or two dollars and you have lost up to $50.

Actus Reus: This is a Latin term loosely translated as "guilty act" or "wrongful act." It refers to all of the components of the crime, except for the state of mind, or *mens rea*, of the culprit.

Advance (as in Advance Fee): The requirement for the victim to pay fees prior to obtaining the benefit, credit, or loan.

Advance Fee Loans: These are promises of a loan even if your credit is bad or you have no credit at all; usually advertised in the classified sections of newspapers, magazines, etcetera. Just because an ad is paid for, it is not the responsibility of the media to verify the legitimacy of the ad.

Affidavit: An affidavit is a sworn, legal document that essentially declares what you are saying is the truth. It may be entered in court as evidence during any proceedings. Most financial institutions have a standard form of affidavit and a commissioner of oaths present to have you swear to the document. An affidavit is the same as a statutory declaration. Often, an affidavit is required before an investigation will commence.

Black Money: Black money is the term used to describe money that has been chemically treated to disguise it from authorities by turning it black. Smuggling money into and out of a country is illegal, and the fraud victim in this case has agreed to become part of this criminal conspiracy.

This scheme has been around for a long time. Generally, one or two of the bills placed on top of the bundles is legitimate and may even be covered with black watercolour paint. This is "washed" by the fraudster with the special chemicals and the bill is revealed. The victim is convinced that the remaining bills have been treated the same way and agrees to purchase the money and ship it to his home country. He is then contacted to purchase the chemicals for an additional fee.

In theory, the bills are treated with a chemical that completely covers any trace of the printing on the paper. The money is then bundled into stacks and put into a suitcase, box, or other container for shipping. Once the money clears customs and arrives at the intended location, the money is then treated with another chemical bath to dissolve the concealing chemicals and turn it back into usable cash.

It does not exist. Although this may be seen in movies and television, those were simply special effects. There is *no such thing* as black money or treated money.

Boiler Room: A term used to describe the telemarketing office where the phone calls originate. Boiler rooms range in size from ten to over one hundred phones and people. The amount of calls generated, the pressure, and high energy that the manager of the boiler room instils in his or her people and the constant need to meet goals contribute to the name.

Certified Cheque: This is a cheque issued by a financial institution verifying that the amount the cheque is written for is available.

Charity Schemes: Unscrupulous criminals will often take advantage of natural disasters or tragic events to defraud people out of their money. They will pose as canvassers for a charitable organization and ask for a donation. Some of these fraudsters will invent names that sound similar to a legitimate organization to avoid a civil suit as well as criminal charges, if caught. Others will even have props, such as photocopies of tax receipts, to assist in carrying out their scheme.

Conditional Discharge: A sentence imposed on a person found guilty of a crime where, upon completion of actions or conditions imposed by the court, there is no criminal record relating to the offence.

Corporate Registry: Corporate Registry is a database of registered corporations for a given province in Canada. The Registry maintains a database showing date of incorporation and the names and addresses of directors and shareholders. The Registry also provides historical information on corporations no longer in business.

It should be noted that the Corporate Registry office does not act as an enforcement agency, provide legal counselling services, supervise the conduct of corporations or non-profit organizations, nor act as a mediator in the case of internal disputes.

Credit Card: A card issued through a financial institution to allow financial transactions.

Credit Card Information: The electronic data stored on the magnetic strip of a credit card or other card device.

Debit Card: A bank card that allows you to withdraw money directly from your banking accounts.

Drop Box: A location where the fraudster tells the victim to mail the cheque or money as part of the scheme. Drop boxes can be leased mail boxes, storage facilities, or offices that have no physical tie to the culprit.

E-Mail: E-mail is an electronic form of communication, which can contain letter-type correspondence, graphic images, or any other data file. E-mail is similar to traditional letter mail in that it is addressed from one individual to another.

E-mail messages usually contain a header, which gives the screen name of the sender, the identity of the Internet access provider, and the return address on the Internet of the individual who originated the message. Depending on how the e-mail software is configured, all or only part of the header information may be displayed to the user.

Internet: The Internet is a worldwide computer network, which connects computers and allows for communications and the transfer of data and information across international boundaries.

Communication via the Internet can take place through many different media, such as accessing a website or sending and receiving electronic mail between computers.

A website is a site (location) on the Internet. Each website contains a home page, which is the first document users see when they enter the site. The site might also contain additional documents and files. Each site is owned and managed by an individual, company, or organization.

Internal Fraud: Internal fraud occurs when employees within a company commit the act of fraud.

ISP and IP Address: An Internet user accesses the Internet from a computer network or Internet Service Provider (also known as an ISP) that connects the Internet user to the Internet. The ISP assigns each user an Internet protocol number, also known as an IP address. Each IP number is unique in that no two computers on the Internet may have the same IP address at any given time.

K.G.B Statements: The term "K.G.B. statement" results from a decision from the Supreme Court of Canada in February 1993, titled R v K.G.B. This decision affected the way in which police officers and prosecutors can deal with adverse witnesses. In the past, a witness who would recant his statement, or refused to testify, was subject only to cross examination by the Crown in an effort to discredit him or her. The previous statement could not be used, as this would violate the hearsay rules of evidence. This decision allowed the admissibility of a previous statement, provided that certain conditions were met.

Condition one dealt with the reliability of the statement. No longer were an officer's paraphrased notes, or a written statement by the witness, enough. The statement must be taken under oath, solemn affirmation, or solemn declaration and the witness must be forewarned of the legal consequences of lying under oath. A videotaped recording of the interview should be made which would allow for the observation of the witness, as if in a courtroom setting.

The second condition would address the necessity of using the witness statement. In previous Supreme Court decisions, necessity usually meant the unavailability of the witness. In K.G.B. the Court deemed that necessity isn't restricted to the availability of the witness and used the guideline of the expectation of getting evidence of the same value from the same or other sources. Therefore, if the witness is recanting or refusing to answer questions, the necessity of using the previous statement is satisfied.[1]

Lien: A Lien is a legal claim against someone's property, or the right to keep or sell someone's property to recover a debt.

Mass-Marketing (*see* **Telemarketing**)

Mens Rea: The Latin term translated as guilty mind. *Mens rea*, in conjunction with *actus reus*, must be present for most criminal charges.

Mooch List: A derogatory term for list of names of people for telemarketers to contact. In fraudulent telemarketing, most of the people on the list have been victimized before and will most likely be taken in by another scam again. Mooch lists are bought and sold to fraudulent telemarketers.

Mortgage Fraud: A type of real estate fraud that generally targets the lender by fraudulently inflating the value of real estate property.

Multi-Level Marketing Schemes (*see* **Pyramid Schemes**)

Mutual Legal Assistance Treaty (MLAT): Mutual Legal Assistance Treaties (MLATs) were established through the 1988 U.N. Convention Against Illicit Traffic in Narcotic Drugs and Psychotropic Substances, and were consistent with the definition of treaty found in the

Mutual Legal Assistance in Criminal Matters Act (Bill C-58). Law enforcement agencies informally share investigative information across the border within the legal limits of both countries, and much information can be handled in this way. The legal limits include the constitutional, privacy, and security safeguards in place in both countries. The *Mutual Legal Assistance Treaty* between the United States and Canada and domestic legislation in both countries provide a framework for each country to obtain information for the other on formal request. *MLAT* requests, for example, form the basis for search warrants allowing the recipient to obtain the evidence requested.

Formal *MLAT* proceedings can consume valuable time and resources for those at both ends of the process. Offenders can sometimes delay proceedings or get information about the evidence being gathered against them by challenging *MLAT* requests. Some forms of assistance are not presently available under the *MLAT* and domestic legislation. There appears to be uncertainty in the law-enforcement community about when *MLAT* requests are necessary and when they are not, which can result in using them when they are not needed.[2]

Nigerian Letters: The term applied to letters, e-mails, and faxes asking for assistance in taking money out of a country. These types of scams did not necessarily originate in Nigeria, but with the growth of the Internet and e-mail, the initial flood of letters initially had a Nigerian connection. These letters are also referred to as advance fee letters or West African letters. The originator of the letter can now be located in Nigeria, Amsterdam, or anywhere else in the world.

Pinhole Camera: A small camera placed above a false PIN pad used to record a fraud victim entering their personal identification number. Some cameras can be wired into the PIN pad or can be used remotely to record the data entered.

Pitch: The offering or type of scheme such as investment pitch, recovery pitch, or travel pitch.

Ponzi Schemes: A scheme targeting investors to put money into an investment that has no real or limited product.

Prize Pitch: A prize pitch is a scheme where the fraudster tells the victim that they have been selected to win a prize or have a choice between several luxury prizes such as vehicles, cash, or jewellery. The victim must pay a processing or handling fee prior to obtaining the prize. The victim fails to be awarded the big prize but is compensated with a smaller, cheaper prize. In a legitimate contest, you do not have to purchase a product to qualify for a prize.

Property Offenders: Generic term to mean criminals that commit crimes in relation to property. These crimes include theft, break and enter, damage to property, etcetera.

Probation: A penalty imposed by the court that requires a guilty offender to abide by certain conditions. Probation can be part of a larger sentence and can last up to three years; however, it does not include serving time in jail.

Pyramid Schemes: Also known as multi-level schemes. This scheme is based on recruiting new investors to insert new money into the scheme, with the promise that as more investors are recruited you move up the pyramid to where you eventually become the beneficiary of the investments. Investors recruit new investors who put their money into the scheme, but no new money is created by the product or company. The only ones to benefit are the originators of the scheme, while those at the bottom of the pyramid lose their money. Before investing in a multi-level company, take the time to do your research. Remember, all pyramid schemes are illegal in Canada.

Real Estate Fraud: The term used to encompass two types of fraud involving real estate: mortgage fraud and title fraud.

Recovery Pitch: If you have been victimized through a previous scheme, you may be contacted by someone offering to recover your lost money. This will usually require some cash from you to help defray the costs to your "saviour."

Restitution: Compensation or re-payment for a loss.

Robbery: The theft of property with the addition of violence or threat of violence.

Scripts: Scripts are the prepared offering that the telemarketer will use once he/she has made contact. They are designed to catch your attention and to convey as much information in as short a space as possible. In fraudulent telemarketing, they are also used to stop the telemarketer from deviating too much and providing too much information.

Shoulder Surfing: A generic term where the fraudster, or an accomplice, surreptitiously watches a victim enter their personal identification number when completing a debit card transaction.

Spam: The term used to refer to the unsolicited e-mails and purchase offers made on the Internet.

Spoofed: The term used to mean a false website of a legitimate company. The site will look valid, but may have small flaws, such as spelling mistakes. The site generally requires the victim to enter personal information in order to verify that the company has the correct data.

Sucker List (*see* **Mooch List**)

Skimming: The term used to obtain information and data from the magnetic strip of a credit card or other card device.

Skimming of Cash: The theft of a small amount of cash from a larger fund. Usually the amount is small enough to go undetected.

Telemarketing: The generic term for mass marketing. Telemarketing is used by legitimate companies and organizations or by fraudulent operators.

Theft: The unauthorized taking of another person's property without consent. Theft does not involve violence.

Title Fraud: A type of real estate fraud that generally targets a home owner by transferring title of property or imposing a lien against the property.

Travel Schemes: These are similar to a prize pitch scheme. By filling out ballots at a trade show you may be contacted offering a free vacation. They will ask you to provide your credit card number or cash to hold the vacation for you. However, the vacation is not forthcoming. The information that you provide may also be sold and you may end up on a "mooch" or "sucker" list. These are not the same as agreeing to attend a seminar for a vacation time-share where you spend a weekend at a resort if you listen to a sales presentation.

NOTES

Chapter 1: The Construction of a Fraud

1. The Criminal Code of Canada, 2007.
2. Tavris, Carol and Elliot Aronson, *Mistakes Were Made (But Not by Me): Why We Justify Foolish Beliefs, Bad Decisions, and Hurtful Acts* (New York: Harcourt Trade Publications, 2008).
3. Originally authored by Alexander Pope in *Essays on Criticism.* The actual phrase is "A little learning can be a dangerous thing." The phrase has been modified on numerous occasions, and used to act as a warning to those who make decisions based on insufficient knowledge or information.

Chapter 3: Telemarketing Frauds

1. PhoneBusters website: *www.phonebusters.com.*
2. 2004 International Conference on Identity Theft discussion paper.
3. Schulte, Fred, *Fleeced!: Telemarketing Rip-Offs and How to Avoid Them* (Amherst, NY: Prometheus Books, 1995).
4. Cialdini, Robert B., *Influence: The Psychology of Persuasion* (New

York: HarperCollins Publications, 2007).

Chapter 4: Loan Schemes and Advance Fee Frauds
1. PhoneBusters website: *www.phonebusters.com.*

Chapter 8: Nigerian/419 Frauds
1. Leacock, Stephen, *Sunshine Sketches of a Little Town*, New Canadian Library (Toronto: McClelland & Stewart Ltd., 1989).

Chapter 13: Real Estate Fraud, False Charities, and Outright Lies
1. First Canadian Title website: *www.firstcanadiantitle.com.*
2. "Mortgage Fraud," Service Alberta Consumer Tipsheet: *www.servicealberta.gov.ab.ca/895.cfm.*

Chapter 14: Who You Gonna Call?
1. Interpol website: *www.interpol.int.*

Appendix: Investigator's Tools for Fighting Fraud
1. Fairbairn, Steve, "U.S.: Canada's a Telemarketing Fraud 'Haven,'" March 2, 2004.
2. PhoneBusters website: *www.phonebusters.com.*
3. Equifax website: *www.equifax.com/EFX_Canada.*
4. United States Postal Inspection Service website: *www.usps.com/websites/depart/inspect/missmore.htm.*
5. FINTRAC website: *www.FINTRAC.gc.ca/FINTRAC-canafe/.*

Glossary
1. Skeet, Detective Brian, "Calgary Police Service Operational Project Plan — K.G.B. Statements," Calgary Police Department report, April 25, 1995.
2. Department of Justice website: *www.justice.gc.ca/en/dept/pub/wgtf/headings.html.*

BIBLIOGRAPHY

Beare, Margaret. *Criminal Conspiracies: Organized Crime in Canada.* Andover, U.K.: International Thompson Publishing, 1995.

Cialdini, Robert B. *Influence: The Psychology of Persuasion.* New York: Harper Collins Publishers, 2007.

Financial Investigations and the Tracing of Funds. Boulder, CO: Paladin Press, 1990.

Iannacci, Jerry and Ron Morris. *Access Device Fraud and Related Financial Crimes.* Boca Raton, FL: CRC Press, 2000.

Katz, Leo. *Ill-Gotten Gains: Evasion, Blackmail, Fraud, and Kindred Puzzles of the Law.* Chicago: University of Chicago Press, 1996.

Leacock, Stephen. *Sunshine Sketches of a Little Town.* New Canadian Library series. Toronto: McClelland & Stewart, 1989.

Peterson, Marilyn B. *A Guide to the Financial Analysis of Personal and Corporate Bank Records,* Third Edition. Glen Allen, VA: National White Collar Crime Center, 2002.

Shulte, Fred. *Fleeced!: Telemarketing Rip-Offs and How to Avoid Them.* Amherst, NY: Prometheus Books, 1995.

Silverstone, Howard and Michael Sheetz. *Forensic Accounting and Fraud Investigation for Non-Experts*. Toronto: John Wiley & Sons, 2004.

Tavris, Carol and Elliot Aronson. *Mistakes Were Made (But Not by Me): Why We Justify Foolish Beliefs, Bad Decisions, and Hurtful Acts*. New York: Harcourt Trade Publications, 2008.

Thompson, Deborah. *Greed: Investment Fraud in Canada and Around the Globe*. New York: Viking Press, 1997.

OR RELATED INTEREST

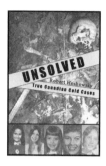